HYDERABAD

Hyderabad

A city of hope

edited by

MALVIKA SINGH

ACADEMIC FOUNDATION
NEW DELHI

www.academicfoundation.com

First published in 2011
by

ACADEMIC FOUNDATION
4772-73 / 23 Bharat Ram Road, (23 Ansari Road),
Darya Ganj, New Delhi - 110 002 (India).
Phones : 23245001 / 02 / 03 / 04.
Fax : +91-11-23245005.
E-mail : books@academicfoundation.com
www.academicfoundation.com

Cataloging in Publication Data--DK
Courtesy: D.K. Agencies (P) Ltd. <docinfo@dkagencies.com>

Hyderabad : a city of hope / edited by Malvika Singh.
p. cm.
ISBN 13: 9788171888849
ISBN 10: 8171888844

1. Hyderabad (India)--History. 2. Hyderabad (India)--Description and travel. 3. Hyderabad (India)--Social life and customs. I. Singh, Malvika.

DDC 954.84 22

Typeset by Italics India, New Delhi.
Printed and bound in India.

For

BILKEES I. LATIF

Contents

Introduction

MALVIKA SINGH

The journal SEMINAR turned fifty in the year 2009. At that time we decided to bring out themed 'compendiums' from the vast treasure of material that the monthly had published over the five and more, decades. As part of that ongoing project, Academic Foundation have reproduced six special issues of SEMINAR, as a set of individual books, that celebrate the historic and famed cities of Delhi; Bombay, now Mumbai; Calcutta, now Kolkata; Madras, now Chennai; Hyderabad and Lucknow. We are delighted that this work will be accessible to a wider audience of Indians as well as visitors to India, who would want to share and experience the many special, personal and individual insights into the life and times of these cities, based on memories, on hitherto unspoken behind-the-scenes stories, some full of joy and others that lament the change, all of which are woven together in an extraordinary tapestry.

My gratitude to Rituraj and Sanu Kapila for having recognised the merit of these carefully crafted mini compendiums, and for reproducing them with much care. My thanks to all the writers who participated in the issues of SEMINAR, making them lively, unusual and substantive. To my colleagues at SEMINAR, my sincere thanks for supporting the many SEMINAR related 'ventures' like this one!

A city of hope

HARSH SETHI

HYDERABAD, like so many other feudal capitals, evokes images of charm and romance, a grandeur and splendour woven with legend which over the years has continued to inspire contemporary folklore. Popular renditions of the city, much like those of its counterpart city in the North, Lucknow, reminisce about the syncretistic Hindu-Muslim culture, a Ganga-Jamuni *tehzeeb*, and an elite drawn across denominational divides that left behind not just iconic wonders like the Charminar, the Chowmahalla and the equally wondrous palaces and *baradaris* but a fusion cuisine marked for its distinction and the quaint speech, Deccani Urdu.

All these descriptions, staple fare in tourist brochures, are to a point true, but as the late C.V. Subba Rao, chronicler of the radical underside of the city, reminds us, beyond the glories of the Nizami era, buildings, pearls and the delectable *kachi biryani* and *mirchi ka salan* or *baghare baingan*, 'these images are part of a self-perpetuating mythology created by the literate', and 'it is now necessary to transcend the barriers created by inherited images.' Not only is contemporary Hyderabad, a six million plus agglomeration, more and different from the erstwhile capital of the Asaf Jah dynasty, we need to revisit its history to grasp both the energy and tensions marking the populace and its popular culture. Equally, without understanding the relations between the city and its hinterland, more extractive than synergistic, we may miss out on its future.

It is often forgotten, particularly in elite accounts, that Hyderabad was a princely state, one which had to be forcibly incorporated into the Indian Union. The late entry of modern civic politics in an overwhelmingly feudal and courtly environment meant that the intermingling among the elite was rarely matched at popular levels. The inability of the Congress party to play an open role meant that public political space was taken over by the Muslim Majlis and its Hindu counter, the Arya Samaj. Further, the decision of the last Nizam, Osman Ali, to seek an independent destiny in the fading days of the Raj, in part egged on by 'communal' Muslim organizations, contributed to a deepening of the divide between the minority Muslim and majority Hindu populace. Finally, the developments post-accession left a vast section of the city's Muslim underclass resourceless, bereft of the earlier patronage of the Nizam and Muslim nobility, and ghettoized. Unsurprisingly, as Ashutosh Varshney so tellingly captures in his *Ethnic Conflict and Civic Life*, Hyderabad soon emerged as a riot-prone city, a distinction now fortunately fading away.

Alongside the undoubted contributions of the Nizams, and ministers like the Salar Jung's, or the English in the setting up of the twin city of Secunderabad, modern-day Hyderabad, as the capital of Andhra Pradesh, has been transformed by substantial infusions of capital, both material and intellectual, in the post-independence era. Site of important public sector units such as the BHEL, major defence establishments (DRDO), CSIR labs like the Centre for Cellular and Molecular Biology, academic centres like the Central and Osmania Universities, as also research institutes like the Administrative Staff College of India, NIRD, ICRISAT, and more recently the Indian School of Business, the National Institute of Information Technology or the Law School, just to name a few, Hyderabad today is a vibrant megapolis, attracting vast numbers of young professionals for both employment and skill enhancement.

Equally of note is the role of the Telugu film industry and media, which over time have created a regional pride and culture, one which draws on not just the Nizami past but equally on the resources pumped in and the preferred aesthetic by the erstwhile landed gentry of the Reddys and Kammas. It is instructive that the Film City on its outskirts today attracts as many visitors as do the historical wonders of Charminar and Golconda Fort.

Little, however, had prepared the city and its denizens for the dramatic developments of the last two decades, both the building boom with its flyovers and commercial complexes surpassing the opulence of similar establishments elsewhere, and the spectacular rise of a regional political party, the Telugu Desam, as the principal challenger to the Congress. Other than shaking up the political establishment, the TDP, in particular the former chief minister, Chandrababu Naidu, attempted to position Hyderabad as the centre of the new economy, based more on computers, pharmaceuticals and bio-genetics than manufacturing industry.

Accompanying the major infrastructural boom has been the creation of a new corporate culture. Hyderabad not just pioneered the advent of the corporate, super-speciality hospital, it was the first city to comprehensively computerize its administration, not just in record keeping but also in the provision of municipal services through the e-sewa. It has even successfully replaced the earlier system of providing mid-day meals in municipal schools through part-time *anganwadi* workers by involving corporate foundations using centralized mechanized kitchens to supply hot, hygienic food in sealed containers through a fleet of container trucks, an unusual example of corporate social responsibility and public-private partnership. The longer term social implications of attempting to create a sanitized, middle class haven in what was once a sleepy city remain to be seen, but for the moment the efforts at re-invention seem to have generated an angst

– of a feeling of exclusion among the less privileged and a nostalgia for the earlier *adab* among the elite.

Equally noteworthy have been the changes in the concerns and orientation of its Muslim underclass. For long ghettoized in the old city, concentrated either in old industry as craftsmen or unskilled service providers, the community was seen as stuck in the past, captive to communal leadership. Both the opening up of job opportunities in the Middle East and the steady growth of modern education, in particular English and computers, have today resulted in a far more materially secure and confident community. Unlike commonplace assertions, an increasing proportion of young Muslim girls, even if *burqa*-wearing, are today working in call centres and the BPO industry. True, Hyderabad is still seen as prone to communal appeals, including those of *jehadi* organizations, but as even a cursory examination of the local Urdu press reveals, the aspirational figures among the young are more tennis players like Sania Mirza than the leaders of Al Qaeda.

For all its vibrancy, there is little escaping the undercurrent of tension as the city continues to gobble up resources – both land and water – at a frenetic pace, in the process changing land use patterns, destroying local water bodies, and displacing both people and employment. Hyderabad today is sitting on a powder keg – the militancy of Maoist groups in the countryside matched by growing impatience of the urban underclass, unwilling to reconcile to the ostentatious display of wealth and consumption. And despite the TDP under Naidu facing a debacle in the last elections, the political class seems to have learnt few lessons.

Like all large cities, Hyderabad too displays many faces, with people inhabiting many worlds simultaneously. There are the glories of the past – the buildings, the crafts, the food and the tehzeeb. There is the vibrancy of the present, new modes of wealth creation and consumption, increasingly involving a cosmopolitan workforce. What shape this will take remains uncertain, but the city still retains its soul and generates fierce pride among its resident *mulkis* and migrants.

Even if somewhat frayed, in part more myth and memory than fact, there is no gainsaying the languorous grace and welcoming spirit, just what makes Hyderabad so special. This volume provides tantalizing glimpses of a city and its people, the glory of the past and the energy of the present.

Importance of the global

SANJAYA BARU

THE North-South Road on either side of the Charminar, we know, ran from the banks of the Musi to the hill on which the Falak Numa Palace was later built. The West-East road began at the majestic fort of Golconda but ran all the way to the prosperous port of Machilipatnam. The significance of this road in the history of Golconda cannot be underestimated.

Golconda, and later Hyderabad, is one of the few landlocked urban centres of this subcontinent that reached great heights of prosperity without a major river system or a port next to it. But that is strictly not correct, for Golconda and Hyderabad had the port of Machilipatnam linking them to the world outside. The road connecting the two was the umbilical cord that linked Hyderabad to the Andhra coastline and from there to global markets, contributing to the region's prosperity for several centuries.

In his impassioned narration of a love story centering around a Hyderabadi princess and a British official, novelist and historian William Dalrymple (2002) draws from archival material to tell us that: 'The road from Hyderabad to the port of Masulipatam was one of the most beautiful in the Deccan.' Of course, it had to be a beautiful road for on it had travelled for centuries bullock carts and horse carts laden with precious stones and highly valued commodities.

Historians are familiar with the vital strategic role of the Machilipatnam port, also known as *'Bandar'*, the Persian word for port. But long before the Persians and the Europeans arrived at Bandar, the Hindu kings of the Satavahana dynasty set forth across the waters from the port of Masalia, later Masulipatnam. In his little known but well-researched account of India's maritime history, Rear Admiral K. Sridharan (1982) records the maritime prowess of the Andhras during Satavahana rule from as early as 1st century AD.

According to Sridharan: 'That the Andhras maintained a fleet is proved by incontrovertible numismatic evidence. The coins minted during the reigns of Pulamayi and Yagnasri (and King Yajna Satakarani around 200 AD) show, on the obverse, representation of sailing ships with two masts.' A ship-building industry developed at Masulipatnam and the Satavahanas forayed deep into East Asia, leaving their cultural imprint as far as Vietnam.

Historians tell us that peninsular India was very much a part of the active maritime trade across Asia, from China to the Persian Gulf, from times immemorial. According to Ken McPherson (2004), along with various ports on the western coast of the Indian subcontinent, Masalia on the east cost (identified as Masulipatnam) was listed in *The Periplus*, the writings of an unknown Greek visitor to India in 1st Century AD, as a port visited by ships from Egypt and the Persian Gulf crewed by Greeks, Egyptians, Arabs and Persians.

Among the goods exported from here to the West were grain, timber, metals, gold, silver and copper coinage. According to McPherson: 'From this early period one of the most unique characteristics of South Asian trade until the eighteenth century AD is evident. Put most simply, South Asia exported a greater value of goods than it imported, with the result that huge quantities of gold and silver flowed into the subcontinent.'

In his masterly survey of maritime India in the 17th century, historian Sinnapah Arasaratnam says: 'A new element in the trade of Coromandel, and what gave Masulipatnam a special place among Coromandel ports, was the forging of trade links with the West – with Gujarat, the Persian Gulf and the Red Sea. This Persian connection was strengthened by the adherence to the Shiite sect of Islam by the Golconda rulers and nobility. This gave them favoured treatment in Persian ports and brought in a substantial Persian merchant migration to settle in the port and the country.

'At the beginning of the century Golconda had emerged as an Indian Ocean port, looking eastwards and westwards. Golconda rulers, anxious to develop their trading ambitions, fostered friendly relations with the Portuguese. With the rise of Masulipatnam, Golconda Muslims and domiciled Persians became another of the Bay of Bengal's itinerant merchant communities.' (p. 50) Textiles, rice, iron and steel, tobacco, indigo and diamonds were the major export items, while imports included Persian silk, horses, coffee, dried fruits, almonds, rose water and coined specie.

Masulipatnam, later called Machilipatnam, developed further as a maritime gateway to the Deccan under Sultan Quli Qutub Shah-I. Golconda in the centre of the peninsula and Machilipatnam along the East Coast became the two most important urban centres of the Deccan in his time. What is interesting about the growing maritime activity of the Golconda kingdom was that it was not just local resources that fed this activity, but the fact that the state's institutional and infrastructure support enabled it to emerge as a maritime state.

There appears to have been a certain entrepot character to Machilipatnam's role in the region's mercantile activity. This was almost entirely because of the enlightened outward-looking nature of the Golconda rulers, and the security they offered to trade and enterprise.

The global was, without doubt, an essential part of Golconda's prominence in its heyday as the seat of power in the heart of India.

The arrival of the Europeans in the waters around India, however, disrupted the indigenous links of maritime trade in the Indian Ocean waters. Trade from and to India passed increasingly into the hands of European traders – the Portuguese on the West Coast and the Dutch on the East, to begin with. Golconda's prosperity was also linked to the West Coast with the Portuguese reaching deep across the peninsula to Golconda. On the Coromandel Coast the Dutch were first challenged by the French and then by the British, who finally held sway.

Nayan Chanda (2007) tells us, in his masterly *tour d'horizon* of globalization how European merchants bought and sold diamonds from the Golconda mines and the bed of the Krishna River through their ports on the West Coast. Chanda tells us, from correspondence of European traders available in archives, the story of Isaac Ergas who would take customers' orders, much like any shop keeper today, in his offices in the Italian port of Livorno for the sale of Golconda diamonds. These orders were sent by hand over sea from Livorno to Lisbon and from Lisbon to Goa, and by road from Goa to Golconda. And, as he tells us, 'If everything went well – and the ship did not sink in a storm – customers receive the diamonds a year or two later!' Hindu traders along the Konkan Coast then bartered the diamonds for corals or other valuables.

These popular accounts remind us that the landlocked fort of Golconda, and its successor urban centre of Hyderabad, was actively linked to the maritime trade of both the East and the West Coast. It required not just the availability of diamonds along the Krishna River and the rocks of the Deccan but the administrative acumen of the Golconda rulers to build a centre of great wealth and prosperity based on trade with distant lands.

Historians are familiar with the great European battles for control over Machilipatnam. First came the Portuguese, and then came the Dutch. They were followed by the French and finally came the British. By the late 18th century the British established full control over the Bay of Bengal after annexing Machilipatnam from the French. By the 19th century when Hyderabad was connected by rail with the presidency towns of Bombay and Madras, the importance of Machilipatnam declined.

However, the growth of modern education and industrialization from the end of the 19th century and through the early part of the 20th century ensured that Hyderabad was one of the few non-British centres of development before independence. The local and the global in the long history of Hyderabad's evolution worked together to ensure the city's prosperity and growth over the centuries.

The control of European interests over the Coromandel trade and the establishment of British imperial control over peninsular India meant that the presidency towns of Calcutta, Madras and Bombay became more important to India's maritime trade. This contributed to the decline and collapse of Machilipatnam and cut its highly productive links with Hyderabad. Not only did maritime trade shift to the presidency port towns but also the rail links between Hyderabad and Madras and Bombay ended Machilipatnam's maritime importance.

More importantly, the division of India into British India and Princely India may have also weakened Hyderabad's links with the outside world. During the era of the last Nizam, Hyderabad did see some industrial activity with the growth of textiles and other industries, but much of this was either based on public investment or investment by expatriate capital, especially Marwari enterprise. Hyderabad's pearl trade was one of the few remnants of its glorious maritime past, and it remains a reminder of the city's links with Asia to our East.

There once was a Hyderabad!

MOHAN GURUSWAMY

ON the morning of 13th September 1948 five infantry battalions and an armoured regiment of the battle hardened Indian Army under the command of Maj. Gen. J.N. Chaudhry entered the princely state of Hyderabad, over a year after independence and after the patience of the new Indian Union was tested beyond endurance. The Nizam of Hyderabad like the Maharaja of Jammu & Kashmir too entertained notions of an independent state and had so far managed to avoid accession. In the meantime, the Nizam sought to widen the issue by moving the United Nations, took the advice and assistance of Pakistan, and began stockpiling arms. *The Times*, London, on 9th August 1948 reported that the Hyderabad army was strengthened to 40,000 and supplies of arms were being received, presumably from Pakistan. The Prime Minister of Hyderabad, Mir Laik Ali, boasted that 'If the Indian government takes any action against Hyderabad, 100,000 men are ready to fight. We also have a hundred bombers in Saudi Arabia ready to bomb Bombay!'

Within the Nizam's realm, militant Razakars led by Kasim Razvi had stepped up their campaign of terrorizing Hindus and whipping up religious sentiments among the Muslims. Within five days the 'police action', actually a military operation, was all but over and the Hyderabad army commanded by Maj. Gen. El-Edroos formally surrendered. The Indian Army's 'police action' was as violent as it was swift. It killed 1373 Razakars and captured 1911. In addition the Hyderabad State Army lost 807 killed and 1647 captured. The Indian Army's losses were never officially revealed but a figure of less than 10 killed is commonly accepted. It was a sudden and crushing end to a movement that had vowed to hoist the Asafia flag on the Red Fort.

At the time of India's independence, Hyderabad was the largest Indian princely state in terms of population and GNP. Its territory of 82,698 sq miles was more than that of England and Scotland put together. The 1941 census had estimated its population to be 16.34 million, over 85% of whom were Hindus and with Muslims accounting for about 12%. It was also a multilingual state consisting of peoples speaking Telugu (48.2%), Marathi (26.4%), Kannada (12.3%) and Urdu (10.3%). Its diversity and broad heritage could be seen in the historical monuments at Ajanta, Ellora and Daulatabad in Marathawada, Bijapur, Bidar, Gulbarga, Anegondi and Kampili in Karnataka, and Warangal and Nagarjunakonda in Telangana.

Hyderabad city's history goes back to the 11th century when the Kakatiya kings of Warangal built the fort that later became famous as Golconda. Mohammed Quli Qutab Shah founded the capital city that we now know in 1590. Quli Qutab Shah was quite a romantic and first called the city Bhagyanagar after his Hindu born Queen Bhagmati. Bhagmati later took the name Haider Mahal and hence Hyderabad. Haider Mahal also inspired him to pen the immortal lines: '*piya baaj pyaala piya jaaye na, piya yakthil jiya jaaye na.*' This romanticism suffused the spirit of Hyderabad through most of its existence.

Hyderabad not only had its own army, but also its own railways, airline, postal service, broadcasting network and currency. The Nizam and his court ruled over it with the British Resident keeping a close and watchful eye over everything. The British Army also had a permanent garrison, just in case the 'faithful ally of the King Emperor' was found lacking in faith. Incidentally this regiment, the 13 Hyderabad consisting of Ahirs from Mewat, was raised by Lord Wellesley, later the Duke of Wellington who won everlasting renown at Waterloo. After accession, 13 Hyderabad became the 13 Kumaon, whose C company won lasting fame in 1962 for its heroism at Rezang La.

As can be imagined it was a Muslim dominated state. Typically in 1911, 70% of the police, 55% of the army and 26% of the public administration were Muslims. In 1941 a report on the civil service revealed that of the 1765 officers, 1268 were Muslims, 421 were Hindus, and 121 others, presumably British, Christians, Parsis and Sikhs. Of the officials drawing a pay between Rs 600-1200 pm, 59 were Muslims, 38 were 'others', and a mere five were Hindus. The Nizam and his nobles, who were mostly Muslims, owned 40% of the total land in the kingdom. Quite clearly it was too much of a good thing for so few and the time for its end had come.

The Asaf Jah dynasty came into being in the waning years of the Mughal Empire. Mir Qamruddin, a Muslim general of Indian origin, was first appointed Governor of the Deccan in 1707. He was called the Nizam-ul-Mulk. He returned to Delhi soon after as uncertainty and turmoil overtook the house of Babar. Qamruddin, after a brief stint as the Mughal *wazir*, returned to the Deccan in 1723 to carve out an independent domain for himself. He was now Asaf Jah I. On his death in 1748, his second son and a grandson, who secured the support of the French and British respectively, contested the succession. The French won this time, but in 1761 they were all but beaten by the British in the Carnatic wars. In 1798 Hyderabad came under the dominance of the English when Asaf Jah II entered into a Subsidiary Alliance with the East India Company, which made sure that Hyderabad remained under the Nizam's rule, but under their guidance.

As can well be imagined there was absolutely no political activity in the kingdom for most of this period. The faithful ally remained just that while the British waged war on the Marathas, Sikhs and then, by introducing the Doctrine of Lapse, gobbled princely state after state. Even the 1857 war passed Hyderabad by. The first stirrings began in 1927 when the Majlis-e-Ittihad-ul-Muslimeen was formed to unite various Islamic sects for 'the solution of their problems within the principle of Islam', and to protect the economic, social and educational interests of the Muslims.

In 1933 an association of *mulkis* or local born Hindus and Muslims called the Nizam's Subjects League was formed as a reaction to the continued domination of non-mulkis in government, even though most of them were Muslims. This was soon to be known as the Mulki League. It was the Mulki League that first mooted the idea of a responsible government in Hyderabad. In 1937 the Mulki League split between the more radical elements who were mostly Hindus and the more status quo inclined. This led to the formation of the Hyderabad Peoples Convention in 1937, a prelude to the establishment of the Hyderabad State Congress the following year. With this the movement for political and constitutional reform picked up momentum.

The Hyderabad State Congress agitation coincided with a parallel agitation led by the Arya Samaj and Hindu Mahasabha of V.D. Savarkar on Hindu civil rights. To a large extent the interests of the Congress and Hindu organizations coincided. This put them squarely against the Majlis that was now led by Bahadur Yar Jung who was also the founder of the Anjuman-i-Tabligh-i-Islam, a proselytizing Muslim organization whose prime activity was the conversion of Hindus. Bahadur Yar Jung was a charismatic figure who became popular among the Muslims. He also had the ear of the Nizam, Osman Ali.

The main thrust of Bahadur Yar Jung was to establish that Hyderabad was separate from the rest of India and that it should be declared a Muslim state. The Majlis also considered British style parliamentary democracy as unsuitable to India in general and Hyderabad in particular. Bahadur Yar Jung summed this up very succinctly: 'The Majlis policy is to keep the sovereignty of His Exalted Highness intact and to prevent Hindus from establishing supremacy over Muslims.'

The Majlis still exists as a formidable political force with a strong presence in Hyderabad's old city area. The party has been winning the Hyderabad parliamentary seat since 1967. The strong presence of the Majlis in Hyderabad contributed to the rise of RSS, and the BJP today has a formidable presence in Hyderabad and surrounding areas. In the recent months the BJP has been actively espousing the formation of a Telangana state comprising of the Telugu speaking districts of the erstwhile Hyderabad state. Ironically the Majlis is also wedded to this cause.

The leadership of the Congress took more nationalist overtones after the arrival of Swami Ramanand Tirtha on the scene. Tirtha hailed from Gulbarga, now in Karnataka, and as a young man became a *sadhu*. He became President of the Hyderabad Congress in 1946 and attracted around him several young men who rose to prominence in independent India. Foremost among these was P.V. Narasimha Rao. Others were former Home Minister and Maharashtra Chief Minister, S.B. Chavan, former Karnataka Chief Minister Veerendra Patil, and former Andhra Chief Minister M. Channa Reddy. By doing so, Tirtha transformed the Congress from a party dominated by Marathi speakers and Arya Samajis into a broad-based organization representing the diversity of Hyderabad.

Even as the Congress was gaining strength, the Communists were also active in the Telugu speaking areas. They captured the Andhra Mahasabha that was formed in 1921 to represent the interests of the Telugu speaking people in 1942. Unlike the Hyderabad Congress, which took its cue from Mahatma Gandhi and launched a movement for democratic rights in the state to run parallel to the Quit India movement, the Communists joined hands with the Majlis to support the Nizam, who being a faithful ally of the British was fully immersed in the war effort. When World War II ended, the Communists, now following the militant line of B.T. Ranadive, took to the path of armed revolution. It is said that when they went to Stalin for help in 1948, he took one look at the map and decided that armed insurrection was impossible to sustain in landlocked Telangana. The CPI was accordingly advised to seek other ways of coming to political power.

The advent of the Indian Army brought in its wake great changes that were sought ever since political activity began in the state. The Muslim elite soon found itself marginalized and many migrated to Pakistan. Others like Ali Yavar Jung made a smooth transition into the new order. A new bureaucratic elite was rapidly installed even as the Communist insurrection was being quelled. The Nizam soon came to terms with the new circumstances and became the Rajpramukh of the newest state of the Indian Union. Nothing reflected the handing over of the baton better than the transition in the Secunderabad Club seen in its picture gallery of past Presidents.

The Club was for long the citadel of power, prestige and privilege in the state and always had a senior British officer as its President. Maj. Gen. El-Edroos, C-in-C of the Hyderabad State Army, became its first non-British President in 1947. In March 1949 he made way for Maj. Gen. J.N. Chaudhry, Military Governor. A galaxy of prominent Hyderabadi's, a number of whom were top civil servants, followed Chaudhry. Since the last decade or so businessmen from the coastal Andhra region have started appearing on the gallery. The times have changed; Hyderabad and the pictures truly reflect this!

The story of Hyderabad, which is also of how a state became a city, doesn't end here. The States Reorganization Bill of 1956 saw the Marathi speaking areas go to Maharashtra, Kannada speaking areas to Karnataka, while Hyderabad city and Telangana were absorbed into Andhra Pradesh. Now with the proposed emergence of a Telangana state – a real possibility – Hyderabad may regain some of its lost cosmopolitan character.

The soul of Hyderabad

BILKEES I. LATIF

WHAT is the soul of Hyderabad? Is it the Ganga Jaumni *tehzeeb*, as it has often been called with some justifiable pride? To those of us of this city, it is much more – the caring, the warmth, the special bonding between people of varied origins, both within Hyderabad and the surrounding Telangana areas. It is a feeling of respect, for *sharafat*, recognizing the decency and good values in another, and thereby being a true 'Hyderabadi'. There is a saying in the Telugu language, *athiti devo bhava*, a guest is like a god, and so it has been.

Through the centuries the ethnic Telugus of the region have intermingled with people who have come and been made welcome to this region of the Deccan. The fusion has brought about a special composite Hyderabadi culture that has evolved between its Telugu population and the Mughals from the North of India with whom Hindus of the Kayasth community came in the 16th century, and occupied important posts in the state. There was a further influx of Turkish and Persian scholars, artists, craftsmen and traders who came between the 16th and 19th centuries, invited by the rulers to embellish the forts, tombs and other structures. This interaction and mingling amongst those of different regions and lands also led to the emergence of a beautiful language, Urdu, with its colourful locally spoken Hyderabadi Urdu or *Dakhni Boli* which often includes an element of humour at one's own expense. Parsees, Buddhists and Jains as well as Hindus and Muslims are all a part of this Hyderabadi composite culture, which is one of understanding, humour, respect and caring that goes back a long way.

What brought about this special Hyderabadi ethos, this innate 'soul' of Hyderabad? As early as 1000 BC, Pliny recorded that those of this region were a strong people with a large army that included elephants! The Deccan region has had a record of great rulers since 236 BC when a small kingdom was established by the Satavahana kings, and thereafter came the dynasties of the Kakatiyas, Chalukyas, Vijayanagara Kings and later of the Adil Shahi, Barid Shahi and Qutb Shahis, thus creating multiple influences through the centuries. When the Buddhists arrived they were treated with respect and thereafter several of the queens became Buddhist, though the kings remained Hindu. Over several centuries the Buddhists illustrated the great caves of Ajanta, with the most beautiful paintings depicting the life of Lord Buddha. Incidentally, after centuries of lying in oblivion, it was the Muslim ruler Mir Osman Ali Khan, the last of the Nizams, who was instrumental in getting the Buddhist caves reopened and restored with foreign expert guidance in the 20th century.

Great temples for pilgrimage, famous diamond mines, and international trade attracted people from many regions. There was contact with distant lands through coastal trade that included the export of precious stones, and printed textiles, especially of the famous chintz that was so popular with the ladies of Rome and further into Europe. The beautiful Dakhni style of miniature painting, the famous kalamkari handpainted textiles depicting the Persian tree of life as well as scenes from our Ramayana are equally a legacy of this fusion. Shipbuilding was another important activity. The British, Dutch, Portuguese and French established trading centres and factories, and unfortunately also benefited from the internecine warring between neighbouring rulers who kept jostling for power.

Between the 10th and 11th centuries AD, one of the greatest rulers of the region was Krishna Deva Raya II. Among the outsiders who came at the time were also Muslim traders. An especially sensitive gesture of this king towards his Muslim subjects was seen when they came with other subjects to pay obeisance to him as their ruler. Being aware that Muslims would only bow to God or their holy book, a Quran was placed on a table next to the throne. They bowed before the holy book, and thus also paid homage to the ruler. Strangely, many of the Hindus chose to wear the Muslim style of pajamas, as well as a *kulah* as headgear, and to use the *salaam* for greeting as the Muslims did.

By the 16th century, from 1512 to1687 AD, the Turkoman Qutb Shahi Sultans ruled this kingdom of Golconda stretching from the Narmada river in central India to the Tungabhadra river in the South, and from the Arabian Sea to the Bay of Bengal. They were great builders who also supported both mosques and temples for worship. The fourth ruler Ibrahim, learnt Telugu and married a Hindu princess named Bhageerathi. He patronized Telugu literature and poetry and appointed a Telugu poet named Addanki Gangadhara Kavi as Poet Laureate. Within a few decades when Golconda became over-populated, the city of Hyderabad was built nearby between 1598 and 1601.

Writers and travellers who visited and wrote glowing accounts about the state included Marco Polo, Nicolo Conti, Duarte Barboza, Athanasium Nikitin, Bernier, Tavernier, Abbé Carré and Thevenot. They described it as the finest city in the East, a city of gardens and a centre of free trade. Marco Polo, speaking of the textiles manufactured in this region in the 13th century said, 'In this kingdom are made the best and the most delicate buckrums and those of the highest price. In sooth they look like the tissues of a spider's web. There is no king or queen in the world but might be glad to wear them.' Warangal carpets, Nanded muslins and Paithani material also had their excellence of design, fineness and durability. The Persian Ambassador who came on a mission to the Qutub Shahi King of Golconda in 1603 and returned only in 1609 took with him, among other gifts, a piece of Kamquab brocade that had taken five years to weave on the looms of Paithan.

Diamonds mined in the state were then brought to Golconda where thousands of men were employed to polish them. These included the Kohinoor, now in the crown of the British monarch, as well as the Orloff, the Hope, and other famous diamonds. Only recently I had a query from Ron Winston regarding the old diamond mines. His father Harry Winston had bought the famous Hope Diamond of Golconda, which was said to have brought sorrow to those who possessed it. Harry Winston donated it to his nation, and it is now the most visited item at the Smithsonian Museum in Washington DC.

There is something romantic in the air of Hyderabad with its lakes, white-domed buildings, the rugged rocks of the Deccan and its beautiful multi-coloured sunsets. The Golconda Fort is where the Qutb Shahi Sultan sat on the terrace, listening to the voice of the singer Taramati, wafting from her *Baradari* across the hills. Premamati, the other favourite, is said to have danced on a set of wires stretched right across these hills till she reached the terrace of the fort. Today the Baradari is once again a cultural centre where singers perform.

The city of Hyderabad was built in an area where Prince Quli Qutb Shah, the heir apparent of the Sultan, used to visit his beloved, a dancer named Bhagmati. When he became the Sultan he is said to have made her his queen with the title of Haider Mahal. He named the city Hyderabad, and built its main monument, the Charminar, on the spot where they first met. At a nearby palace there was a large dining hall where delicious meals were served free every day to the poor. Not far from it is the Mir ka Daira, the graveyard established by Mir Momin. A great prime minister, he designed the city of Hyderabad around the Charminar in a parallelogram with houses for the rich and poor, schools, a hospital, nine and seven storied palaces with piped water from artificially created lakes and gardens for coolness along the Musi river with the maintenance of temples and mosques funded by the ruler.

An outstanding queen of this era was the Sultan Quli Qutb Shah's beautiful daughter, Hayat Bakshi Begum, who was not only the daughter of a king but the wife of another king and then the mother of a future king. Widowed when she was only twenty-one in 1626, she ruled the kingdom ably as her son was still a child. It is said that when her son Abdulla was born, it was predicted that if his father, the Sultan Mohammad Qutub Shah, set eyes upon him before he became twelve years old, the Sultan would die. The boy was kept away from his father, though both father and son yearned for each other. When Abdulla was almost twelve his father accidentally saw him, and soon thereafter passed away.

The queen appointed two able Brahmins, Akkanna as the prime minister and his cousin Madanna as a minister, believed to be ancestors of Narasimha Rao, our late prime minister. In 1685 when Aurangzeb laid siege to the city, this brave queen went out, beyond the walls of the fort, to the emperor's camp. She made a deal with him proposing that if his eldest son Prince Mohammad married her granddaughter, the daughter of the ruling Sultan, he would be designated as heir apparent and the next ruler of Golconda. And so the siege was lifted. The last Golconda ruler, Abul Hasan, was known as Tana Shah, a colourful character. Yet it was through his support that the dying Kuchipudi dance form was revived, as he made a grant to the village that provided support, and saved it for future generations. Tana Shah was also particular about pundits and pujaris being fed on special days.

There is an account about Tana Shah and the great temple dedicated to Sri Rama at Bhadrachelam on the banks of the Godavari river. This ancient temple was rebuilt at a cost of six lakh rupees by Ramadas Gopanna, the nephew of Akkanna, the prime minister. As no funds were available to repair the temple, he took the required amount from government revenues. When this offense was discovered, he was arrested. He prayed to Lord Rama for help and it is said that Sri Rama and his brother Lakshmana appeared before the Sultan one night, gave him a bagful of coins equivalent to the amount taken, and enjoined him to release Gopanna. The Sultan not only set Gopanna at liberty but thereafter made an annual grant to this temple which his successors, the Nizams, continued to give in the form of jewellery.

On a visit to this temple I heard the head priest relating that as long as the Nizam Mir Osman Ali Khan was alive, he sent an annual offering of a priceless pearl necklace to this temple even when he was no longer the ruler.

In 1687 Aurangzeb attacked Hyderabad again. It was only by bribing a traitor within who opened a side door that his troops finally poured in. The women in the fort jumped into a huge well and killed themselves rather than be captured alive. Hyderabad was then looted and its palaces were razed to the ground by the invaders. Mir Qamruddin Khan was sent from Delhi, appointed Subedar with the title of Nizam-ul-Mulk. He later assumed the further title of Asaf Jah in 1725, the founder of the Asaf Jahi dynasty of the Nizams who ruled Hyderabad thereafter till 1948. He brought with him Sagar Mal the recently orphaned son of his late prime minister whom he brought up almost as his own, as well as numerous Kayasths. They, as well as their descendants, served as dedicated and efficient bureaucrats and statesmen of Hyderabad. They strictly observed their own traditions and religion, but also adopted much of the Hyderabadi lifestyle and ways, thus further enhancing its culture.

Towards the end of the 19th century, in 1884, the sixth Nizam, affectionately known by the people as Mahbub Ali Pasha, the Beloved, established a constitutional monarchy. Towards the end of his reign, on Monday the 28th of September 1908 the rains poured down without a break for over 48 hours. The heavy downpour, breaking all barriers, swept onwards thundering down the Musa river over the bridges and deep into the lanes and streets of the old city. The waters surged ahead washing away all life before its wild onslaught. The Nizam went every day to the area till the waters subsided, and did whatever was needed for those whose homes had been swept away. He stood in the river with the priests, pujaris and maulvis to calm the waters with the chanting of prayers and performing of pujas and soon the rains abated.

An interesting tale about the Nizam Mahbub Ali Pasha refers to a trip that he made to Manikpur near Homnabad, where he visited a revered *sadhu*, the descendant of the great Manikprabhu Maharaj. The sadhu and the Nizam found themselves in harmony, and the sadhu proposed that they exchange souls while meditating. They sat together quietly in meditation and the Nizam who previously had a terrible carbuncle on his back was amazed to find that it had healed! Maharaj then gave the Nizam a sacred thread to wear, and it is said that from then onwards the Nizam acquired certain powers of healing and was able to cure victims of snakebite.

Mahbub Ali Pasha did not have this kind of rapport with the British. At the Durbar in 1903, Lord Curzon had invited the rulers of the states and decided to garland each royal invitee, the first being the Nizam. The latter held up the sword that he wore for ceremonial occasions and did not bend his head to receive the garland. The Viceroy then said that he would place the garland taking it over the Nizam's head. Mahbub Ali Pasha was, however, unhappy about the efforts of the British to dominate him, as they had managed to annex the districts of Berar. He replied that as he had come to assure the ruler of his faithfulness, it was proper for him to present his sword which was always available, and thus a permanent symbol of loyalty, rather than his head, which was easily dispensable. Despite the Viceroy's long look, the Nizam stood without bending his head. Finally the Viceroy hung the garland on his upturned and steady sword.

The 7th Nizam, Mir Osman Ali Khan was born in 1886 and became ruler at the age of twenty-five on his father's demise in 1911. The era of modern development in the state began thereafter. The young ruler, well educated by select scholars, was fond of writing poetry. Stylishly dressed, he was at ease with social graces and even enjoyed formal ballroom dancing. He announced that he would be a caring and just ruler.

He issued the Nizam's Asafia creed stating, 'Whatever be the religion of my house and my own personal beliefs, I am, as a ruler, the follower of another religion as well, which must be characterized as "love towards all" because under me live people of different communities, and the protection of their houses of worship has for long been part of the constitution of my state. I do not desire therefore, to injure with narrow-mindedness the susceptibilities of any community or faith, or to distort the practice of my religion in such a manner as to earn the title of a bigot. In my capacity as a ruler, I consider myself an atheist, but in the sense of being without ties as a ruler for or against any religion or community. In that faith, I and my forefathers have taken just pride and will continue to do so.' He started off by building houses for the poor to prevent slums, and constructed artificial lakes and dams for adequate water supply.

There were 32000 temples and 6000 mosques in the state, 11355 Hindu and 5024 Muslim religious institutions, as well as churches, and the famous Sikh gurdwara at Nanded, most of which were given annual grants by the Nizam's government. Hindu officials managed 90% of these temples as well as mosques. There was much criticism of the seventh Nizam for his personal frugality. One of the richest men of his time, he chose to spend his wealth on his state and on various causes rather than on himself. He appointed good administrators and experts such as Vishveshwaraya, and prime ministers such as Maharajah Kishen Pershad, Sir Akbar Hydari, as well as advisors like Imad-ul-Mulk and Faridoon Jung, the latter a Parsi gentleman whose descendants and their families still symbolize the best traditions of Hyderabad, and the closeness and caring that form the soul of Hyderabad.

When the Prince of Wales visited Hyderabad in 1922, the seventh Nizam had special arches erected in the city. The Charminar was decorated with crystals to look like the fabled diamonds of Golconda, with an illuminated outline of the Prince's Feathers as well as of the Nizam's headgear, the *dastar*. Fine fabrics of the state were displayed upon the arches as were examples of the famous Karimnagar silver filigree work, bidri damascene work, lacquer and many other craft. The motto, *Harkat me Barkat Hai*, was emblazoned on the sides. However, though a 'faithful ally' of the British monarch, because of the extensive aid given for World War II, there was nearly a diplomatic 'incident' on this occasion. The Nizam refused to go to the railway station to see off the Prince of Wales. He said that it was not correct protocol for a ruler to go to the railway station to see off a prince.

An oft-related tale is that in 1724, while leaving Delhi for the Deccan, Asaf Jah sought the blessings of a holy man. The saint, about to start his meal, offered the food to Asaf Jah who took a few pieces of the bread. The holy man kept asking him to take more. After accepting seven *kulchas*, Asaf Jah said he could take no more. The saint then gave his blessings and told him that he would be the first of seven of his dynasty to rule the Deccan. And so it came to be, for Mir Osman Ali Khan was the seventh and last Nizam who ruled the dominions of Hyderabad. Sadly, in the last years of his rule, the seventh Nizam did not realize the consequences of the growing power of the Razakars, which brought about such humiliation.

After the state was merged with the Indian Union in 1949 and Andhra Pradesh formed in 1956, the city of Hyderabad was retained as the state capital. Fortunately, the special ethos or soul of the city also remained intact. It was just a few years ago that the previous chief minister of Andhra Pradesh, at a public function, stated that for many decades Hyderabad had been well known abroad because of the achievements of Mir Osman Ali Khan, the seventh Nizam and last ruler of Hyderabad. It was also known in India as a premier state with its own airline, an excellent railway, and good roads throughout the kingdom, which was about the size of France. In the first half of the last century, Hyderabad had established centres of excellence that were outstanding for the period.

In recent years not only major government institutions, but business houses too have been established, increasingly so since Hyderabad now has its own Cyberabad. The influx of people from all over India continues. Hyderabadis still retain their composite culture and cosmopolitan outlook with warmth of hospitality. There is a consciousness of being part of a confluence of varied streams and shared values.

Despite the setback created by the Razakars followed by the severe aftermath of retaliation, the warmth and understanding of the Hyderabadi ethos remains. It has continued despite the times of rioting, and now of bomb blasts, in the historic masjid and park. The people see this as politically motivated destruction, as it has always been. The Hyderabadi closeness and the ganga jamuni tehzeeb remains, even as the fabric of faith gets weakened with each incident. One is bewildered by this deliberate destruction of innocent life that was unknown till recent times and wonders whether a polarity is not slowly creeping in.

Several hundred years ago the saintly Hosain Shah Wali had created the lovely Hussain Sagar lake in just a couple of years. However, most outsiders now feel that Hyderabadis are too laidback in their attitudes. There is some truth in this for the citizens have been putting up with the most terrible stress over 'improvements' and the delayed completion of flyovers. The placid *chalta hai* attitude includes tolerating unpunctuality as well as an acceptance of action to be taken *parson.* This does not mean 'the day after tomorrow', but could be any day or month beyond that! But a sense of humour remains despite the grumbling.

There are many more parks and gardens now, an especially lovely one being the Lotus Pond on Banjara Hill, if one can spray oneself with anti-mosquito repellent before entering. Sadly, the two beautiful lakes, Himayatsagar and Osmansagar, created to provide water by the last Nizam a century back, are being allowed to dry up and it is said that the land will then be sold at high prices for housing. The acquisition of wealth seems to have become all-important. The growth of private and public construction is phenomenal. Earlier, the younger visitors complained that there was little to do in the evenings, but now there are plenty of pubs, shopping malls as well as restaurants, jewellery shops, and some bookshops too. A drive around Hussain Sagar on the lovely Necklace Road takes you to a line of eateries overlooking the lake.

Hyderabadis love to eat, indeed, almost live to eat. Most conversations seem to end with a discussion on food! In restaurants all over town or even if one is walking down a street at dusk, one gets the aroma of saffron and cardamom from a hot *kachi biryani* of fine rice and succulent meat, of which it is said that once eaten it will draw you back to the city for more! Hyderabad food has its own character depicting its composite culture. The food has the flavours of saffron, cardamom and nutmeg from Persia, the rich fried spices in ghee from northern India, enhanced by its basic, piquant, local Andhra ingredients of sour tamarind fruit, curry leaves and hot red chillies in meat, seafood, fowl or crisply fried vegetables and spicy, chilli hot dishes. Chilli hot food is followed with a helping of plain yoghurt and boiled rice as in the deep South to cool down the fiery fumes, and the rich masalas in the baghare baingan and *mirch ka salan* become easy to digest because of the addition of tamarind, so popular in Telengana.

There are certain days of joy, days of prayer, and of community interaction. Ugadi is New Year's day, the first of Chaitra, the first month of the lunar Hindu calendar in spring. The lady of the house gets up before dawn to pray and perform the traditional ceremonies. A special meal must include a symbol of the different *rasas* or flavours of life. So for sourness there is tamarind pulp and grated raw mangoes of the spring season, with a little salt, as well as cane sugar and jaggery as symbols of the sweetness of life. One must take the bitter with the sweet, so the bitter fresh flowers of the neem (margosa) tree are added. If someone finds the taste bitter, it is interpreted as an omen of the bitterness that he will face in the year ahead! During the day there are *pujas* and the main event is in the evening, when an astrologer makes predictions for the following year.

When Surya, the Sun God, moves to the North it is considered a sign of hope and progress and a time for the Sankranti festival, which falls on the 14th of January. Bhogi is the day before Sankranti when the house is spruced up and all the broken or shabby things discarded. Families go on a picnic, and the sky comes alive with multicoloured kites. Milk and rice are boiled to bubble up and overflow in euphoric symbolism, signifying plenty and prosperity ahead. *Chakkara pongal* is a sweet of rice, milk, nuts cooked with ghee for the occasion, as is *bobbatlu*, a half-moon shaped stuffed pastry.

For the Parsis and Muslims of Persian origin, a very special day is Nauroz on 21st March, and again there are six special ingredients of symbolic value that are served and eaten on this day of sharing and prayer. Then comes the Bonalu festival with its Bathkama, the figure of the Goddess Gauramma swathed beautifully with flowers, and the worship of seven sister goddesses. At Holi, friends spray each other with coloured water or powder. Maharaja Kishen Pershad, a popular prime minister, would send to the Nizam and a few special friends, balls of very fine lacquer called *khumkhuma*, each filled with red *gulal* powder and *abeel*, a perfumed white powder. When pressed, the balls would burst, showering perfumed powder to permeate the air around. In years long past, every year on Holi the banjaras of Banjara Hill would come in a large group to the house of my uncle, Nawab Mehdi Nawaz Jung. Young family members would join in as the women dressed in their lovely colourful costumes danced. Taherra Begum and Mehdi Nawaz Jung would exchange token dabs of colour and then serve them special snacks.

Christmas is another day of special prayer when even non-Christians would go to the church. As a young girl, I once went to the grand old Church at Medak, a district not far from Hyderabad. Long lines of villagers came walking in the dark to attend midnight mass, carrying lanterns and singing hymns. The hymns were sung in Telugu and the entire service too was in a language that the people understood rather than in Latin or English.

The Eid-ul-Fitr is a day of special celebration for Muslims. The men go to the mosque for special Eid prayers and then the young people and children go calling on relatives. Each one is served with the traditional sweet *sheer khurma*, made of very fine vermicelli cooked in milk and loaded with almonds and pistachios cut in slivers, and chopped dates. Wrists are dabbed with fragrant *ittar* and *paans* served to every visitor. Often the young are given a gift of money, or an 'Eidi' by their elders, who stay home to receive visitors.

For girls, dressing up in the morning after a bath used to be quite a ritual – wet hair dried over perfumed incense smoke, with the clothes similarly perfumed before being worn. Girls still love to wear the traditional *khada dupatta,* a six metre long material with broad and intricately embroidered borders, worn draped around over a *kurta* and fitted pajama. The traditional *kurti* has a special round opening below the neckline, outlined with the special *zardosi* and *karchob* embroidery. The people of Hyderabad retain their fondness for their traditional jewellery too. But now the young people are also keen on reaching out to the trendy new styles in vogue elsewhere.

Sometimes roles get reversed. Recently, a French woman visitor was so attracted by the lines and style of the men's *sherwani* or *achkan* that she got one made, and it has been greatly admired in Paris. The textiles most sought after have been the Pochampally *ikats*. Though available in town, designers from abroad make a beeline for the little village where the weavers have their looms. Another attraction is the pearls that come from all over in their original soft colours, and are bleached in Hyderabad. They are then sent off to a village where each pearl is wedged into a wooden socket to hold it steady, and a hole pierced in it before being threaded into a necklace.

A person who shared and embodied these special Hyderabadi values was Sarojini Naidu. When her father Dr. Chattopadhyay was invited to work in Hyderabad, he and his family stayed for a long time with their old friend, a very learned man, my great grandfather Sayid Hossain Bilgrami Imad-ul-Mulk. Sarojini grew up in Hyderabad and joined the freedom movement. At an inaugural address at the Nizam College in 1937, she stated, 'More than any responsibility that you have as Hyderabadis is the tradition of unity. In the outer world, where I live and travel, what is known as British India, they exalt the unity that prevails in our city. I always maintain that here, in the State of the Asaf Jahis, there are deep elements of human fellowship. Here, if nowhere else, we have solved the problem of communal unity.

Others have greeted Hyderabad as an example of how Hindus and Muslims can work together in friendship and brotherhood.

'Never be it said of you that, by a single gesture, you have created even a ghost of a suspicion of discord. For the destiny of India is to be determined by the unity of her people. No longer should there be a consciousness of majorities and minorities, that I belong to this community and he to that; for, so long as it persists we are not a nation, we are but a people divided against ourselves. You should show by precept, and by everyday practice, that the questions of the majority and minority communities, of tongues and races, do not exist, that the citizenship of the state can be achieved only when all sections unite for a common purpose.' What she said then applies today as well. Sir Akbar Hydari, an outstanding former prime minister of the state spoke in a similar vein.

Today the race for mammon pervades the atmosphere. The dynamic Andhra with his concentration on earning good money has helped to bring in more business and prosperity. The Gulf-returned Muslims now celebrate weddings in Function Halls, a symbol of success that soon leaves them denuded of all their savings! On the other hand there was the poet Maqdum Mohiuddin with his leftist leanings, whose poems still reverberate in the halls at Sham-e-Ghazals long after he passed away. The sons of the great Qawwal Aziz Warsi who is no more are still in demand, and everyone longs to hear, again and again, his old favourites like Maqdum's *Chameli ka Mandwa*. Yet the Chameli ka Mandwa, a grotto down a lane from the Charminar where once there were creepers and bushes laden with the fragrance of flowering jasmine, is now a bare and dusty corner.

Mir Momin, Maqdum and Aziz are no more, nor are Sarojini Naidu or Akbar Hydari, Maharajah Kishen Pershad, or Salar Jung, now remembered more for his descendant's collection of Objects d'art in a museum than as the great modernizer he was. They have all been a part of the voiceless soul of Hyderabad. Does the rush of the brash race for visible success swamp this Hyderabadi soul, with its elegance and values getting submerged by the glitter? The voices of the poorer boys for whom there is schooling of sorts available, often free, are loud in their insistence on leaving school by the 6th or 7th standard so that they can begin earning, for there is so much available to tempt them. While it is good that jobs are available for the poor and middle class, but the prices of basics such as dal and onion still remain beyond their reach.

Most Hyderabadis prefer to observe from the sidelines. Whether smiling with amusement or saddened and distressed, they still closely bond, as a part of the real Hyderabad. Just as I began to wonder if the soul of Hyderabad is fading away, I came across something heartening in a newspaper. It referred to the endless problems that the state government has been facing about acquiring land from people for road widening in the newer areas of town with their large houses and big business offices. The article then mentioned that in the old city, people of all communities have not only agreed to hand over their much loved small or large properties for road widening to improve the area, but one young member of a highly criticized political party actually handed over two acres of land without any compensation. So, the Hyderabadi warmth and caring that is its soul, still exists. This soul, with its elegance and values must not be drowned in the glitter, the rush and the loudness of the brash race for visible material success.

Bridging two cultures

NARENDRA LUTHER

THE twilight generation of Hyderabadis and its diaspora scattered in five continents, suffers from an acute nostalgia for the twilight period of the city of their origin. One has only to browse the Charminar Connection website to appreciate the depth of their feeling and pride in what they call the *Ganga-Jamuni* composite culture of Hyderabad.

The charm of the old-world ambience was still lingering when I arrived in the city a decade after the integration of the old state of Hyderabad with India in 1948.

The origin of this flavour can be traced back to over four centuries. In 1591, the fifth Qutb Shahi Sultan of Golconda, Mohammad Quli (r.1580-1612) built a city as 'a replica of heaven'. He named it Bhagyanagar, after his beloved Bhagmati. In 1983, the German architect Jan Pieper quoted a chapter and verse to argue that the city was indeed an architectural metaphor for the Quranic heaven.

Hyderabad is to cities what Taj Mahal is to buildings – a monument to love. Both were named to commemorate the respective beloveds – Taj for Mumtaz, Bhagyanagar for Bhagmati. Whereas Taj symbolized a pining for a departed beloved, Bhagyanagar was a celebration of a union of lovers. Taj was to enshrine a resting place for a departed queen, Bhagyanagar to provide living space for her subjects.

Mohd. Quli was the first *saheb-e-diwan* Urdu poet of India. He bequeathed a secular legacy to the city. His poetry also celebrated the monsoon season when the city is at its best. Its onset is officially decreed on 7th June though it often violates that injunction with impunity.

In 1724, the Mughal governor of the Deccan, the first Nizam, became independent and founded the Asaf Jahi dynasty. According to legend a hermit prophesied that his dynasty would rule for seven generations, which indeed it did.

Aurangzeb's hated *jaziya* – poll tax – was never imposed in the South. On the other hand, a broad streak of secularism runs through its history.

In 1805, a Kayasth noble, Raja Bhavani Pershad, built the first Kayasth temple at Rambagh near Attapur. The third Nizam, Sikander Jah, performed the installation ceremony of the idols of Rama, Sita and Lakshmana. He also granted a *jagir* of 12000 rupees for its maintenance.

The population of the state of Hyderabad was predominantly Hindu. Its founding dynasty, Qutb Shahi, subscribed to the Shia sect of Islam. The Asaf Jahis were Sunni. Of the ten highest noble families under them, one was Sunni, five Shia and four Hindu. Out of the Hindu families, two were Deccani, and two from North India – one Kayasth and the other Punjabi Khatri, tracing their ancestry to Todar Mal, Akbar's celebrated revenue minister. This diversity of the ruling elite imparted a distinctive flavour to the Hyderabadi culture.

The British Residency, especially after its completion in 1805, became a powerful source of British influence on a conservative society in various subtle ways including dress, manners, education and living style. Many men of means came out of the walled city and built their residences in the new suburbs around the Residency.

Salar Jung I was the Diwan of the state for 30 years from 1853. In a bid to modernize the administration of a medieval state, he recruited a large number of persons educated in British India. They too brought modern impulses with them.

In 1869 Mehbub Ali Khan became the sixth Nizam when he was not yet three. He was the first Nizam to be educated on modern lines under British supervision. He spoke English and wore western dress. He grew into a dandy and never wore the same dress twice. Unsurprisingly, he had the world's largest wardrobe – some 70-metre long hall with double-storey almirahs.

Old people used to tell me that the worst floods in the city occurred *purson* – the 'day before yesterday'. They meant 1908. In the Hyderabadi lexicon, the term covers all remembered past. To stop the deluge, as advised by some Hindu pundits, Mehbub Ali Khan placated the goddess Bhavani by performing her *arti*. His subjects venerated him.

The seventh – and the last ruling – Nizam, Mir Osman Ali Khan (r.1911-48), was reputed to be the world's richest man of his time. He had no idea of his wealth, not surprising for a man whose personal estate yielded 2.5 million rupees and whose privy purse was five million rupees a year. Besides, in 1919, he published and became the sole selling agent for the six collections of his poems for one guinea each. (Yes, the price was fixed in guineas! It was equivalent to 21 rupees). He was also presented a *nazar* whenever someone was given the privilege of an audience. Every senior official of the state presented him a nazar twice a year – on Eid and on his birthday. The honour of a present of even one mango from his private estate, or a part of his *khasa*-dinner, sent ceremonially to a noble or a randomly chosen subject had to be acknowledged gratefully with a nazar the next day. The minimum amount for a nazar was one gold and 20 silver coins – 24 rupees!

The man who made so much money lived an extremely frugal life. He wore the same cap for years, even when its rim showed stains of sweat and oil. His clothes showed no sign of having been ironed.

Osman Ali Khan inaugurated an era of construction that went far beyond the repair of the city devastated by floods. Apart from the Osman Sagar and Himayat Sagar reservoirs built to prevent floods, and the broad, concrete Pathargatti Bazaar, a number of new buildings came to dot the city and its new suburbs. The Osmania Hospital, the High Court, the State Central Library adorned the new skyline of the city. The jewel in the crown was the Arts College of the Osmania University built in 1938. Its unique feature was that its medium of instruction was Urdu. The students attended class in formal dress – sherwani, pajama and fez cap. Urdu men of letters thronged to the city from all over India seeking patronage from the court and the nobility. Dazzled by its beauty, they called the city *uroos-ul-balaad*, 'bride amongst cities'.

The Nizam's misfortune was political. The country was astir with new political aspirations. In the state, the majority demanded representative, responsible government. The minority Muslim party, the *Majlis-e-Ittehad-ul-Mussalmeen,* countered this majority clamour by demanding that Hyderabad be proclaimed an Islamic state. Its fanatical leader, the Razakar 'Field Marshall' Kasim Razvi, also instigated him to declare independence. That proved his undoing.

In a swift four-day Police Action in September 1948, the Indian Army put an end to this ambition. The Nizam lived through his remaining two decades in isolated glory still issuing *firmans* on petty matters, which were published by a faithful Urdu daily, the *Nizam Gazette.*

While Hyderabad was founded on love, Secunderabad was an offspring of coercive diplomacy. Hyderabad was a quintessential Oriental city renowned for its planning; Secunderabad was a cantonment which grew into a replica of an English town.

The second Nizam signed the Treaty of Subsidiary Alliance with the East India Company in 1798 for his protection, and to be overseen.

Accordingly, the Company sent six battalions and stationed them on the north side of the Hussain Sagar Lake in Hyderabad. Starting as a tented camp, it grew into a cluster of barracks. The import of consumer goods to the cantonment was exempt from customs duty, making trade and commerce more profitable than in Hyderabad. A number of business establishments came up in the area. In course of time, flourishing markets like the Regimental Bazaar and General Bazaar came into being. In 1806, the new township was given the name of Secunderabad after the ruling Nizam, Sikander Jah.

Till 1858, the cantonment of Secunderabad consisted of barracks and huts extending to a distance of about five square kilometres with the artillery in front on the left flank and the infantry on the right.

After the Mutiny of 1857, it was decided to build a fortification for the forces. A mud fort with a circumference of about four square kilometres was completed in 1867 at Trimulgherry and was called the 'Entrenchment'. Its 17-feet high wall was surrounded by a moat. It had four main gates named after famous battles which the British had won in India. In an emergency, the entire European population could be accommodated within the Entrenchment.

The Mudfort Road and Entrenchment Road still exist, but nobody knows about how they got their names or what happened to the original structures. The military hospital and the cellular jail are located within the perimeter of the Entrenchment. Built like a cross with arms in four directions, the jail was nicknamed Windsor Castle.

A shaded avenue from Begumpet to Marredpalle, called the Alexandra Road, divided the cantonment from its civilian appendage. James Street and Kingsway connected it to Hyderabad via Tank Bund. After independence, they were all given Indian names.

Alexandra Road and Oxford Street had the most fashionable European shops. They included Badam Pyle (confectioners), Mapin and Webb (cutlery and crockery), Richard & Co. (goldsmith), Spenser (aerated drinks), John Pile (general stores), Bright & Co. (chemists). John Burton was the most fashionable draper and tailor. A.S. Abdul Khader had a department store. H.M. Hussain had a textile store. J.C.

Pinto ran a bookshop. Raja Deen Dayal finally overtook over twenty European photographers in Secunderabad. The nobility of the old city went there for fashionable shopping. The second son of Nizam VII, Prince Muazzam Jah had his sherwanis stitched at Burton's. When he was there, no one was allowed entry, except European women. He would buy the whole roll of cloth so that no one else would have a similar sherwani.

Percy's was the main western hotel in Secunderabad. At its rear was a popular dance hall. Close to it was the Plaza Cinema with an attached bar. That was the only cinema hall in the country in which one could sip beer while watching a movie. There were a number of other cinema halls on the cantonment side. They showed only English films. Now they are all gone. Two function halls have sprung up in their place.

The King Edward Memorial – now Gandhi – Hospital was established in 1851. Close by was the old Civil Jail. It is now a thriving retail market. When the Secunderabad Railway Station was constructed in 1874, a predominantly Anglo-Indian colony grew up close by in Lallaguda. It was nicknamed 'Little England'. Now it is difficult to see an Anglo-Indian there.

As against Hyderabad where earlier Persian, and since 1884, Urdu was the official language, in Secunderabad it was English. Methodical town planning, better civil administration, greater civil liberties and a broader mix of people from all over India and abroad made it more cosmopolitan than the old city of Hyderabad. To cross the Tank Bund was to go from a medieval to a modern city. Of the many communities that stayed in Secunderabad, two – the Anglo-Indians/Christians and the Parsi – were specially concentrated in Secunderabad.

Christianity came to India in 52 AD with the arrival of the apostle St. Thomas in Kerala. In the following centuries it spread to various parts of India. Niccolao Manucci noted in his *Storia Do Mogor* the considerable presence of Christians in Hyderabad during the 17th century. The ban on the entry of missionaries into British India was lifted in 1813 leading to a spurt in their activities.

The first Vicar Apostolic of Hyderabad was established in 1806 with residence at Secunderabad. Since 1882, there has been a bishop in Secunderabad. Various denominations of Christians became active in missionary and educational work. The Trinity Church in Trimulgherry was the first to be established in 1816 followed by a string of other churches all over Secunderabad.

Schools like St. Ann's Convent established in 1856 have imparted education in the English medium to generations of girls from the twin cities. A number of other schools, both denominational and secular, for boys and girls were also established.

In 1878, Salar Jung gifted his country house to the army for providing a home for the Secunderabad Club. It is now considered one of best five clubs in the country.

Mullah Kavus Bin Rustam Jalal is considered the first Parsi to have come to Hyderabad in 1784. Their knowledge of Persian and English enabled the Parsis to move easily with both the Indians and the British. They became active in commerce and banking, railways and revenue services.

Secunderabad also had a number of modern swanky restaurants. The first Chinese restaurant, Nanking, came up opposite the Montgomery Bar. Both still exist.

In 1945, the British restored an area of 5.6 square kilometres south of Alexandra Road with a population of about 100,000 to the Nizam. To this the Nizam's government added, and established the Secunderabad Municipal Corporation in 1951. In 1964, it was merged in the Municipal Corporation of Hyderabad. It now comprises an area of about 17 square kilometres. A decade later when I became the sole administrator of the Corporation, Secunderabad's distinct superiority in civic standards over Hyderabad was noticeable. Gradually, however, the distinction disappeared.

Some famous names are associated with Secunderabad. Winston Churchill stayed in Bolarum in 1886. Sir Ronald Ross isolated the malaria virus in Begumpet and won the Nobel Prize in 1902. Raja Deen

Dayal the world-renowned photographer had his studio there. The 1997 Miss World, Diana Hayden and the god-man, Chandraswami, also belong to Secunderabad.

The essential difference between Hyderabad and Secunderabad is that the former was a feudal Muslim city, while the latter was a cosmopolitan colonial town. Hyderabad was where the Nizam lived; Secunderabad housed the British Resident who wielded the real power in the state. The Nizam's prime ministers were selected or approved by the Resident before the ruler formally appointed them. Every prime minister first called on the Resident who returned the call. We have a detailed account of the ceremony when Nawab of Chhattari, on his appointment as prime minister, called on the Resident, C. G. Herbert on 30th June 1947.

Hyderabad was out of bounds for the soldiery of Secunderabad. The tiny city, Secunderabad, therefore, provided all amenities for a diverse citizenry. Before the rendition of Secunderabad, as it was called, a meeting was held between the Sub Area Commander of Secunderabad and high officials of Hyderabad on 5th April 1945. It was agreed therein that in the transferred area, 'high standards of services and cleanliness' would be maintained. Also that the Percy's, Montgomery and Whitehall hotels would remain open to visiting army officers for accommodation, concerts and parties. The closing time for bars in Secunderabad, 9.30 pm, would be maintained.

The residents of Secunderabad enjoyed greater civil liberties than those of Hyderabad. The Urdu press in Hyderabad was servile. Any poem written by the Nizam had to be published on the front page of the paper. There was no such obligation observed in Secunderabad where the first English papers were published. When the proposal for the rendition of Secunderabad became known in 1945, a memorial was submitted to the president of the Cantonment Board signed by 551 citizens. That it was signed by different persons in English, Telugu, Urdu, Hindi and Tamil attests to the demographic diversity of Secunderabad. The memorial pointed out that they were 'accustomed to a particular kind of administration, type of life and other conditions entirely different in many respects from those obtaining in Hyderabad. These circumstances pertain to their administrative, commercial and financial interests.' They, therefore, asked for safeguards and a referendum on the issue.

While Secunderabad was somewhat of a homogeneous entity, Hyderabad has grown by stages into a number of suburbs that have fused together over time. Most modern educational and research facilities were located in Secunderabad. There are no open spaces left in the old city while, thanks to the cantonment, Secunderabad still has a number of them. The annual Republic and Independence Day parades are held in Secunderabad. Hyderabad is a political hotspot while Secunderabad shows little political excitement. Hyderabad has a large NRI presence in West Asia; most immigrants from Secunderabad have gone to the United States and Australia.

The Secunderabad Club and the Nizam Club of Hyderabad exemplify the differences between the twin cities. The former is heavily western in its orientation, facilities and in its mixed cuisine. The latter is best known for its Mughlai food. Hyderabad bears the stamp of Muslim culture; the residual flavour of Secunderabad is a mix of Christian and Parsi. However, these distinctions are fast blurring, both having come closer and grown beyond recognition.

In 1991 a new 'triplet' city was born. Christened Cyberabad by its creator Chandrababu Naidu, it represents the new, hi-tech, global face of Hyderabad, its new centre of gravity.

Hyderabad was conceived in the image of heaven. All its gardens and low buildings have been gobbled up by new apartment buildings. Multi-storey malls have sprung up even in the exclusive residential areas. Its arteries are choked, its breath polluted, its heritage all but vanished. The 2.5 billion-year old, fascinating rocks are being recklessly destroyed. Paradoxically, while people's income is going up, their quality of life is coming down.

Nostalgia is for that lost heaven of broad concrete roads, of a low skyline, and of gardens. It is a longing for a world of laid-back life, of courtesies, of *mushairas*, *qawwalis* and *chowki* dinners. It is a yearning for the sepia tones of yesteryear.

I too suffer from nostalgia. I came to this city five decades ago. I still live in Hyderabad, but where is Hyderabad, *O bird of time*?

Diwan Deodi

RANI SARMA

SOME two centuries ago the old city of Hyderabad was dominated by the palaces of the Nizam called *mahallas* or *havelis* and the traditional residences of the powerful nobles called *deodis* (variously spelt *deorhis* or *devdis*) built along the main arteries of the city that radiated from Charminar.

Deodis, which in a broad sense means the 'homes of lords' were fortified residences built with imposing main entrances high enough to let an elephant with an *ambari* pass, tall enclosing walls to afford total privacy to the inmates, and a series of inner courtyards which served the public and private needs of the residents. They had attractive pillared pavilions called *dalans* which were the reception areas, private living quarters for men and women called *mardanas* and *zenanas*, and other sundry buildings like a *diwan khana* where the master held court, a *naubat* khana, from where auspicious music played on special occasions or indicated the time for prayer, the *bawarchi* khana, the kitchen from where cooked food was carried, sometimes under armed guard to the living quarters of the residents, a *tosha khana*, *farrash khana*, *baggi khana* and many similar structures.

The deodis of the very wealthy and the influential nobles were like self-contained townships built in close proximity to the Nizam's palaces. Some of them were so sprawling that they occupied whole blocks, often-times spilling over to the following block as well. Records indicate that there were a few hundreds in the old city at one time, most of which have since been demolished subsequent to the abolition of the jagirdari system in 1949. Today just a handful of them remain in varying degrees of decay.

Prior to its demolition, the Diwan Deodi was one of the most celebrated deodis in the city. Home for generations of diwans it was known for its grandeur and opulence. In a remarkable coincidence unparalleled in history, six members of the same family rose to the position of diwan in the princely state of Hyderabad and all of them lived in the Diwan Deodi. Consequently, for over a century and a half, the Diwan Deodi was the epicentre of power, influence and authority. The location of the deodi itself was a statement of its importance, located as it was on the Charminar High Road, back to back with the Purani Haveli, one of the many palaces of the Nizams.

During that time the deodi saw hectic official activity; officials of all hues and stations like the zamindars, mansabdars, pattedars, vakils, munshis, urzbegees, pairavikars and sycophants besieged it. The Lakkadkot, the *baradari* of the Salar Jungs, a beautiful multi-floored wooden structure built in the middle of a terraced garden overlooking the Musi river, was the venue of many state receptions and banquets.

In its heyday, the Diwan Deodi was like a city within a city, a microcosm of Hyderabad itself; it stretched a whole block, from the Chatta Bazar on one side to the Mir Alam Mandi on the other. Of the six diwans who lived in the deodi, the most prominent were Mir Alam, Salar Jung I and Salar Jung III. Mir Alam was the first diwan of the family (from 1804-08) and he set the family's fortunes on the course to power and fame. His political career, however, was marred by controversy and today he is remembered more for the construction of *sarais*, tanks and a market that he built in and around Hyderabad.

The most illustrious occupant of the Diwan Deodi was the great grandson of Mir Alam and the fourth member of the family to become a diwan, Mukhtar-ul-Mulk Sir Turab Ali Khan Salar Jung I (1829-83). Salar Jung was a statesman par excellence as well as a skilled administrator. Despite inheriting a state steeped in corruption, decadence and anarchy, by the time he was done with it Hyderabad was well on its way to becoming a frontline state in the country. Being a reformer and a man of modern views, Salar Jung borrowed administrative ideas from British India and adapted them to suit the local conditions.

As the co-regent of the child Nizam, the three-year-old Mahabub Ali Khan, he enjoyed enormous powers and was the *de facto* ruler of Hyderabad. In that capacity his main concern was to save Hyderabad from decay and financial collapse that it had slipped into through decades of mis-governance. In striving towards that end he had to walk a tightrope of maintaining friendly relations with the British, and at the same time keeping them at an arm's length to prevent them from interfering in the internal affairs of Hyderabad. He threw his weight behind the British whenever it served the interests of his state; and that was the reason he supported the British during the Revolt of 1857. The British, on their part, realized the importance of having Hyderabad on their side but were wary of the sagacious noble. They held him in respect and treated him with a great deal of deference.

The Diwan Deodi was built, extended, furnished and decorated over a period of a century and a half. The family enjoyed immense wealth and was also very refined and cultured in its tastes. The deodi was so luxuriously furnished and so full of rare objects that visitors to the city, both European and Indian, would request permission to visit it. Around 1905, one such European visitor, Claude Campbell, left a detailed account of the deodi's many attractions, though by that time, we are informed, the deodi was already old and parts of it had fallen into disuse.

The deodi at its height had many grand reception rooms, an extremely well-stocked library, luxuriously appointed guest suites, a *diwan khana*, *mardanas*, *zenanas* and, at a later point, a movie hall, apart from a host of other sundry structures that a residence of a premier noble ought to have. The showpiece of the deodi, however, was the *aina khana*, which meant, literally, the glass house, which was the reception room of the deodi. The aina khana was an open-pillared hall, faced entirely with plate glass. On the ceiling and the columns of this pavilion-like structure, various coloured glasses were arranged in interesting designs in the prevailing Persian style. The aina khana was furnished with a number of gilt chairs upholstered in red velvet, which were said to have graced the court of King George III at one time.

The aina khana was complemented by another glass house opposite to it, which was smaller in size but was similarly decorated with glass. A grand banquet hall connected the two pavilions. Nestled by the three structures was an elegant courtyard, decorated with a large marble fountain and a *hauz*, which was, as a member of the family remembers, large enough to 'row a skiff'. Exquisite European statuary, sculpted in marble and imported from different European countries, stood all around. The reception rooms themselves were screened from public view by red velvet curtains fringed in green and guarded by *Borse ke jawan,* the Arab guards, dressed in their native uniforms.

To the west of the quadrangle and the aina khana was the library which was stocked with many rare books. The library with Shah Jahani multi-foliated arches housed eight thousand manuscripts in Persian, Turkish, Arabic and Urdu, apart from 29,000 printed books! The range of topics covered by the collection is a measure of the mind of the Salar Jungs. There were books on history, archaeology, art, literature, travel, religion, social sciences and many other subjects. Though the major part of the collection was made by Salar Jung III, there was quite a collection of manuscripts and books that he inherited from his ancestors, right from 1656 AD. Some of the Arabic manuscripts were very ancient; one of them, a copy of the Quran dating back to 1283, contained the autographs of Emperors Jehangir, Shah Jahan and Aurangzeb. This fabulous collection today forms a part of the Salar Jung Museum Library and is open to scholars and researchers.

Close to the aina khana to the east was a small room called chini khana, which was an unusual and a most interesting apartment. Its walls and columns were covered in antique china plates, saucers and cups, some of them very valuable; they were fitted into the walls and arranged in various fanciful designs. In this quaint room the family silver plate was tastefully displayed in shelves. It was here that the famous statue of Rebecca, an exceedingly artistic sculpture of white marble sculpted by the Italian sculptor Benzoni (in 1876) stood. Beyond the chini khana to the east was the treasury.

Adjoining this apartment was the formal diwan khana or the durbar hall, arranged in the traditional style with a gold embroidered *musnad*, a *takhat* and canopies on silver poles, where the diwans traditionally held court. Upstairs, above the chini khana were the bedrooms built in the days of Sir Salar Jung. One bedroom in particular was exquisitely furnished in white and gold. It had a cut-glass hand basin and toilet fittings.

A subtle change overtook the otherwise traditional deodi in the early decades of the 19th century. European influence increased at the court and so did the interaction between the Europeans and the Hyderabadi nobility. Prominent citizens began to introduce elements of European lifestyle in their residences, and apartments were fitted to suit western taste. The traditional durbar halls and reception rooms did not suffice; reception rooms fitted with contemporary European furniture had to be added and more western elements like a billiard room, library with English and French literature, guest suites with western toilets and tennis courts came to be introduced. So much so that a European visitor to the Diwan Deodi commented that sections of Sir Salar's Deodi resembled a wealthy Englishman's residence!

If the men's quarters buzzed with official and state activity, the women's quarters were marked by comfort, leisure and ease. The zenana had its own courtyards open to the sky and was equipped with fountains, flowering bushes and pretty *chamans*. The atmosphere in the zenanas was restful and slow-paced. Water tinkled in the fountains and flowering trees like *mulchari* (minusops elengi) and *champa* sprayed fragrance into the air. Women kept birds like *mynas* and *lal munias* for pleasure.

All around the courtyard were rooms, which were skirted with ornamental *dalans*. The central *dalan* was generally the largest and was equipped with a *takhat* and other paraphernalia like a *hookah*, a silver *paandan*, *ittardan*, *gulabposh*, *ugaldan*, a *khasdan* and a water container, which was kept locked when not in use. Guests were welcomed with *ittar* and rose water.

Surrounded by such opulence, seated on an expensive carpet or a low diwan and leaning on *gau takias*, the principal begum of the family presided over the affairs of the zenana with the dignity and grandeur so typical of the Hyderabadi nobility. It was customary for the women of the deodi to pay their respects to the senior Begum when she held court. The married daughters of the family were sometimes provided with separate quarters. The women of the Salar Jung family were known for their strong character and dignity.

The next diwan to rise to fame after Sir Salar was Nawab Yusuf Ali Khan Salar Jung III. However, it is not as a statesman or a prime minister that Yusuf Ali Khan is remembered today but as a collector of art objects. Ironically, he alone is remembered among the long line of *diwans* (for his one man collection of art), while the rest of the family members, including the more able Salar Jung I, is consigned to the history books.

Salar Jung III officiated as a diwan precisely for two and a half years; he did not enjoy good relations with his master, Nizam VII. Unable to keep up with his energetic and extremely able ruler, he resigned soon after being appointed as the diwan. Thus, his career was aborted even before it had time to blossom. What Salar Jung III did not realize at the time was that the loss of his position was to result not only in his political oblivion but also in isolation and neglect.

Shorn of power and influence, neglected by friends and followers, Salar Jung III remained a lonely and tragic figure for the rest of his life.

Yusuf Ali Khan's emotional exile had just started. To add to his woes, his private life did not fare much better either despite his famous charm, wealth and social standing. His name was romantically linked with many beautiful women of the time. Daughters of at least two British Residents were said to have been infatuated by the Nawab. Leila Wellinker, who married David Lean in the later years, was even formally engaged to him for a while. But nothing came of such relationships. Yusuf Ali Khan remained a bachelor all his life.

Salar Jung III was a man starved for company; he sought people, whether he knew them personally or not. The reception rooms of the deodi were packed with visitors; all were welcome. He never sat down to lunch with less than fifty people at his table. Sportsmen, poets, writers, art collectors and strangers gathered in the deodi and enjoyed his hospitality; the conversation at the table was most lively and highly stimulating. Through all that Salar Jung remained aloof and sad, a lonely and restless figure, his eyes searching for the unknown. He paced the corridors of the sprawling deodi restlessly, his footsteps echoing hollowly in the empty halls, as if haunted by the ghosts of his illustrious ancestors, opening and closing cupboards and examining his art-pieces with unseeing eyes. People who knew him remember his 'caged animal walk'.

It was at this time that he started to indulge in his passion for collecting artifacts. Perhaps it was an obsession that sustained him through the years of loneliness. He was like a man possessed. All his wealth went into the acquisition of beautiful objects. Room after room in the deodi came to be stocked with art objects that arrived from all over the world, some not even opened from their protective packing at the time of his death. His reputation as an art collector spread; catalogues poured in through the mail and art dealers besieged him. He had agents in all the important cities of the country who scoured the markets for valuables. He was also known to frequently purchase from Christy's and Sotheby's. He travelled abroad often in pursuit of his beloved artifacts.

The sprawling deodi with its large halls started to look like a warehouse; the art pieces were strewn everywhere, on tables, chairs and in every conceivable corner; he did not let the servants dust or re-arrange his collection, partly for fear of theft and partly for fear of breakage. He had a wonderfully retentive memory; at any point he could recall where a particular object was kept. A time came when the deodi could not take in any more objects; they had to be stored in other palaces. The collection included all the sundry bric-a-brac that crowded the Nawab's life, from the armies of tin soldiers he played with as a child to a priceless collection of jade; antique bronzes, marble statuary, textiles, Far Eastern art, an eclectic assemblage of paintings, jewellery, ivory and rare illuminated manuscripts, some dating back to the Mughal period. Some of these are of great value, some ordinary and others both childish and idiosyncratic.

The Salar Jungs, as a family, were known for their philanthropy. Whenever and wherever the Nawab showed himself, he would be mobbed by hordes of petitioners; he would receive all the petitions with equal courtesy and his secretary would process them. He gave away generously even when he was aware that some petitions were not genuine. He was a lover of music and literature and a keen sportsman; a part of the present airport in Begumpet was the private polo ground of the Salar Jungs. Yusuf Ali Khan was an ace polo player, and among those with whom he played the game were Sir Winston Churchill and the renowned player, Shah Mirza Baig, who was originally from Hyderabad.

He was deeply religious but was no religious bigot. During the month of Muharram, when the Shia community of Hyderabad went into mourning to commemorate the martyrdom of Hussain at Karbala, Yusuf Ali Khan would hold *mushairas* and have famous artists visiting the city render *gazals* to a private and select gathering in his deodi.

The events that shook Hyderabad to its very core in the turbulent years of 1947-49 did not spare Yusuf Ali Khan either. There were rumours that the jagirs were to be abolished. The Nizam's rule had already been set aside. He did not know what was to become of his beloved art collection. His desire to set up a museum with his possessions had not yet taken shape. The death of his friend Sarojini Naidu had saddened and depressed him. One day in the month of March in 1949, he went to see Sardar Vallabhbhai Patel. What transpired between the two gentlemen is not known. The Nawab shut himself in his room for days, and died soon after, a lonely man.

Immediately after the Nawab's death, the valuables from the deodi were photographed, documented, sealed and put in the vaults of the Imperial Bank at Sultan Bazaar. Subsequently, over many days, the contents of the deodi were auctioned. Retainers pulled out clothes, suits, shoes, scent bottles, cutlery, crockery, vases, sheets, floor spreads, lights and tents from the tosha khana, mez khana and the farrash khana. The beautiful deodi was relentlessly stripped. There were four ivory chairs, presented to Tipu Sultan by the French government, which were still in packing at the time of the Nawab's death. They were purchased at a cost of Rs 80,000. These chairs are now on display in the Salar Jung Museum.

To institutionalize the Nawab's art collection, the Government of India created the Salar Jung Museum. The bulk of the exhibits for the museum were drawn from the personal collection of Salar Jung III, and the museum initially was housed in the deodi itself. In 1968, the museum shifted to a new building specially built for that purpose. With the descendents of Salar Jung choosing to live elsewhere, the deodi fell into disuse for a few years and was subsequently declared unsafe for habitation. It was finally demolished in the early seventies. With its mindless demolition, Hyderbad lost one of the grandest of deodis in the city and the memories of two centuries, not only of the family but also of the city itself.

Restoring heritage

WILLIAM DALRYMPLE

SIXTY years ago, a full four months after British rule had come to an end in India, the Nizam of Hyderabad, then the richest man in the world, was still refusing to sign up to join the new Indian union.

Sir Osman Ali Khan firmly believed that there was no reason why Hyderabad should be forced to join either India or Pakistan. His state, which had remained semi-independent within the framework of the Raj, had income and expenditure equal to Belgium, and exceeded that of twenty member states of the United Nations. His personal fortune was more remarkable still: according to one contemporary estimate, it amounted to at least £100 million in gold and silver bullion, and £400 million in jewels. Many of these came from the Nizam's own Golconda mines, source of the Koh-i-Noor and the Great Mogul Diamond, then the largest ever discovered. He also owned one of the Islamic world's great art collections: libraries full of priceless Mughal and Deccani miniatures, illuminated Korans and the rarest and most esoteric Indo-Islamic manuscripts.

Partly because of this extraordinary wealth, the Nizam was always feted by the British as the most senior prince in India, and given clear precedence over all his rivals. For over three centuries his ancestors had ruled a state the size of Italy – 82,700 square miles of the Deccan plateau – as absolute monarch, answerable, in internal matters at least, to no one but himself. Within this area, the Nizam could claim the allegiance of some fifteen million subjects.

Nor was his reputation just limited to India: during the years leading up to the Second World War, the Nizam was also regarded by many as the leading Muslim ruler in the world. A few years earlier, in 1921, the Nizam's two sons had been sent to Nice where they married the daughter and the niece of the last Caliph of Turkey. Abdul Majid II had recently been expelled from the Topkapi by Attaturk and sent into exile in Provence. As part of the marriage arrangements, the Caliph had nominated the Nizam's son as heir to the Caliphate, so uniting the supreme spiritual authority of the Muslim world with its greatest concentration of riches. The dynasty seemed unassailable.

Yet even in the late 1930s, more far-sighted observers realised that the Nizam's world could not last. 'He was as mad as a coot and his chief wife was raving,' I was told by Iris Portal, the sister of Rab Butler, who had worked in Hyderabad before Independence. 'It was like living in France on the eve of the Revolution.'

'All the power was in the hands of the Muslim nobility. They spent money like water, and were terrible, irresponsible landlords, but they could be very charming and sophisticated as well. They would take us shooting, talking all the while about their trips to England or to Cannes and Paris, although in many ways Hyderabad was still living in the Middle Ages and the villages we would pass through were often desperately poor. You couldn't help feeling that the whole great baroque structure could come crashing down at any minute.'

One day in the late 1930s, Portal had been taken to see some of the Nizam's treasure which was hidden in a secret vault in one of the palaces. She had befriended the Caliph's niece, Princess Niloufer, who led her down some stairs, past a group of Bedouin Arab guards, and there at the bottom was a huge underground garage, full of trucks and haulage lorries. The trucks were dusty and neglected, their tyres flat and sinking into the ground. But when the two ladies pulled back a tarpaulin, they found that the trucks were full of gems and precious stones, pearls and gold coins. The Nizam lived in fear of either a revolution or an Indian takeover of his state, and had equipped the lorries so that he could get some of his wealth out of the country if the need came. But then he lost interest in his plan, and left the lorries to rot, incapable of driving anywhere, but still full of their consignment of jewels.

The disintegration of the state, and the dispersal of the wealth of the Nizam, is one of the 20th century's most dramatic reversals of fortunes. After months of failed negotiations, India invaded Hyderabad in 1948, replacing the Nizam's autocratic and despotic rule with parliamentary democracy. Twenty-six years later it abolished the Nizam's title – along with those of all the other princes – removed their Privy Purses and made them subject to crippling new wealth taxes and land-ceiling acts, thus forcing them to sell most of their property.

Mukarram Jah, the Nizam's grandson who succeeded the old man in February 1967, quickly found himself enmeshed in debts and financial chaos. He had inherited a ridiculously inflated army of retainers: 14,718 staff and dependants, including no less than 42 of his grandfathers' concubines and their 100 plus offsprings. The Chowmahalla palace complex alone had 6000 employees; there were around 3000 Arab bodyguards from Sudan and the Yemen, and 28 people whose only job was to bring drinking water; 38 more were employed to dust the chandeliers, while several others were retained specifically to grind the Nizam's walnuts.

For all the rococo Once-Upon-A-Time-There-Was-A-Princess-Who-Lived-In-A-Huge-Palace quality of the Nizam's world, by 1967 everything was in a state of severe disarray: the Nizam's garages, for example, cost £45,000 a year to keep in petrol and spare parts for 60 cars, yet only four vehicles were in working condition, and the limousine supposed to take the Nizam from his coronation broke down on the way to the reception. Officially, two thousand people a day were fed from the Nizam's kitchens, yet it was discovered that several local restaurants were also secretly being supplied with food at the Nizam's expense.

Most debilitating of all was the legal wrangling initiated by the several thousand descendants of the different Nizams, almost all of whom claimed part of Jah's inheritance according to their rights under Islamic personal law: by 1973, 476 legal heirs of the Sixth Nizam and 1945 descendants of the Fifth had filed suits or claims of various sorts. Jah's father – who had been passed over in the will – and his aunt, led the legal challenge. Even getting the smallest sum to live on proved difficult for the new Nizam: his vast inheritance had been distributed between 54 different trusts, the control of which were disputed. From the beginning, despite nominally inheriting one of the world's greatest fortunes, he was forced to sell jewellery and other family heirlooms to keep solvent.

Eventually in 1973, frustrated and disgusted by the weight of litigation and the bitterness of the family in-fighting, Jah took off from Hyderabad, and relocated to a sheep farm in Perth, Australia. There His Exalted Highness, the Rustam of the Age, the Aristotle of the Times, The Victor in Battles and the Leader of Armies donned blue overalls and spent his days tinkering under the bonnets of his cars, or driving bulldozers, JCBs and heavy earth moving equipment around the Australian bush. As his biographer John Zubrzycki memorably put it in *The Last Nizam*: 'His grandfather composed couplets in Persian about unrequited love. To Jah's ears there was nothing more poetic than the drone of a diesel engine.' Visitors frequently mistook him for an electrician or a sheep sheerer. Jah was not bothered, 'Abu Bakar [his ancestor, the first Caliph] was a shepherd,' he told one interviewer. 'So I see no reason why I shouldn't be one too.'

Jah soon sacked most of the 14,000 staff he left behind in India, and divorced his first wife, the sophisticated Turkish princess Esra who, perhaps understandably, saw no reason why she should move to a remote and isolated Australian sheep station. Over the following two decades Jah married a succession of four subsequent wives. One, a plump, blonde Australian secretary named Helen Simmons, died of AIDS in 1989, which led to the intimate details of the Nizam's marriage being splashed across the front of the Australian tabloids. All five of the marriages added to Jah's ever growing pile of litigation, as each successive wife demanded fabulous sums in alimony.

In his absence, Jah's unsupervised Hyderabad properties were looted and his possessions dispersed by a succession of incompetent, dishonest or unscrupulous advisors. When Jackie Kennedy came to Hyderabad on a private visit a few years later, she recorded her impressions of this collapsing and leaderless courtly world in a private letter to her friend, the art historian Mark Zebrowski: 'We had an evening with the old noblemen of the court,' she wrote, men with long white hands transparent like alabaster, who recited Urdu poetry to us... The hereditary Prime Minister of the Nizam, I think his name was Ali Pasha, had his own lime grove: such in-bred trees that their leaves are translucent and the *paan* made with them unlike any other… There were three ancient classical musicians playing in the moonlight, and the noblemen were speaking of how it was all disappearing, that the youth didn't appreciate the ways of the old culture, that the great chefs were being taken by the Emirates… This over-civilised world – you knew it was too rarified to survive…

'The evening was profoundly sad. My son John told me the next day that the sons of the house had taken him to their rooms, because they couldn't stand the classical music – and had offered him a tall glass filled with whisky and had put on a pornographic cassette in the Betamax, and the Rolling Stones on the tape deck. They wore tight Italian pants and open shirts, and all the while their fathers, on the terrace in beautiful Sherwani [frock coats] were speaking of how sad they made them. Ali Pasha's son had disappeared a year before, on a motorcycle, because he didn't like the marriage that had been arranged for him…'

In 1997, when I first visited Hyderabad in the course of the research for my book *White Mughals*, the loot of the Nizam's property was nearly complete. Most of the easily moved valuables that the Nizam had left behind in India had disappeared or been sold by the mid-1970s; but the drawing rooms of the city were still buzzing with stories of how precious jewels, manuscripts, Louis XIV furniture and even chandeliers from the Nizam's palaces were available on the market, for a price. It was unclear how much, if anything, of the proceeds ended up in the pocket of the exiled Nizam.

Meanwhile his different properties were decaying. Many palaces were sealed by orders of different courts. Those which weren't were quietly sold off or encroached: between 1967 and 2001, the Chowmahalla shrunk from 54 acres to 12, as courtyard after courtyard, ballrooms and whole stable blocks, and even the famous mile-long banqueting hall were all acquired by real estate developers, who demolished the 18th century buildings and erected concrete apartments in their place.

One day I visited the huge Victorian pile of the Falaknuma Palace, just to the South of the city. The entire complex, which lay above the town on its own Acropolis, was empty and semiruinous, with every window and doorway sealed by red wax. Wiping the windows, I could see cobwebs the size of bedsheets hanging from the corners of the rooms, like something out of an Indian reshoot of *Great Expectations*. The skeletons of outsized Victorian sofas and armchairs lay dotted around the parquet floors, their chintz entirely eaten away by white ants, so that all that remained was the wooden frame and the springs. Vast desks lay on rotting red carpets covered with a peppering of huge holes as if they had been savaged by some monstrous outsized moth.

Beyond were further long, gloomy corridors, leading to unseen inner courtyards and *zenana* wings: mile upon mile of empty arcades, now quite empty but for a pair of lonely *chowkidars* shuffling around with their *lathis* and whistles. Outside stretched acres of scrub flats, once presumably soft green lawns, dotted here and there with kitsch statues of naked cupids, waterless fountains, and paint-flaking flagpoles leaning at crazy angles. It was the most melancholy sight imaginable: a derelict *Ruritania*, once magnificently opulent, now almost absurdly decayed and neglected.

Then, in 2001, I happened to be on another research trip to Hyderabad when I received a phone call from a friend. The Nizam's first wife, Princess Esra, had unexpectedly appeared in the city after an absence of three decades. With her, she had brought the celebrated Indian lawyer, Vijay Shankardass.

According to my friend, Esra had recently met her ex-husband for the first time in thirty years at the wedding of their son Azmet in London. Esra was shocked to hear of the state of Jah's affairs: to meet his debts he had been forced to sell off his beloved Australian sheep farm and to flee his creditors, had relocated to a two room flat in Antalya in southern Turkey. A partial reconciliation followed, and Esra was given the authority by Jah to try and save something for their son and daughter before what little remained in Hyderabad disappeared too. Among her initiatives, she was intent on settling the many outstanding law cases, opening up the palaces, and leasing Falaknuma to a hotel chain. The principle city palace, Chowmahalla, she planned to turn into a museum.

Begun in 1751, Chowmahalla was one of the finest royal residences in India and a central location for *White Mughals,* but I had never been able to get inside to see it. After some negotiation, I was allowed to accompany the princess as she visited, and so happened to be there at the breaking of the seals of some rooms which had not been opened since the death of the previous Nizam in 1967.

What we saw that day was extraordinary. After Jah had decamped to Australia, much of his property had been left untouched, as if in the palace of Sleeping Beauty. The jewels and most easily lifted art treasures had long gone – in some cases, the empty silk-lined jewel cases still lay scattered along the corridors – but many less easily purloined treasures remained.

In one underground storeroom, thousands of medieval scimitars, swords, helmets, maces, daggers, archery equipment and suits of armour lay rusted into a single metallic mass on a line of tressel tables. In another lay album after album of around 8000 Victorian and Edwardian photographs of the Nizam's household, covered in a thick cladding of dust. An entire and unique set of 160 harem photographs dating from 1915 lay loose in a box. On the walls, dynastic portraits were falling out of their frames, while scattered in the white ant-ravaged book shelves were 800 illuminated Korans. In one room were great mountains of princely dresses, *patkas, chaugoshia* and *salwars*, drawers of Kanchipuram silk saris, and one huge trunk containing nothing but bow ties. There were long lines of court uniforms as well as whole sets of harem clothes once worn by the Nizam's favourite wives. Elsewhere were discovered almost 8000 mostly incomplete dinner services, one of which alone had 2600 pieces.

In a different palace, King Kothi, were found three rooms stacked floor to ceiling full of the Nizam's dynasty's complete correspondence since the mid 18th century. When the archivists had been sacked in 1972, the entire archive had been stuffed into the rooms and sealed: ten and a half tonnes of tatty, disordered and uncatalogued historical documents. Other rooms were stacked equally high with crates of French champagne – now undrinkable – and apothecaries boxes full of Victorian tinctures, as well as huge piles of soap and shampoos.

It looked a complete mess that day; an impossible task to even begin to sort out. Every one of the palaces was riddled with termites and white ants: sprung floors were rotting; ceilings were collapsing, furniture falling apart. Nothing had been painted or maintained for over thirty years.

Yet remarkably, six years later, the Chowmahalla is now open to the public and a thousand visitors a day are streaming through. A massive conservation project, unique in India, has sorted through, catalogued and restored the best of what remains. The result is little short of incredible.

In the story of how the Nizam's inheritance was saved, the urbane figure of Princess Esra's lawyer, Vijay Shankardass, plays the most extraordinary role. Shankardass is the only lawyer alive who has both chambers in Lincoln' Inn and a practice in Delhi. He is renowned for being as clever as he is honest, a rare conjunction of qualities in the modern Indian legal system. As the man who represents Salman Rushdie, he is also celebrated for his courage and tenacity.

I met him in the largest suite of Hyderabad's grandest hotel, which he has occupied intermittently since beginning work on the Nizam's estate in 1996: 'I was contacted by Princess Esra's lawyers in England,' he told me, 'and asked if I could intervene in trying to sort out the jewellery trusts which the last Nizam had set up.

Esra had been badly cheated by her previous lawyer in Bombay who had run off with a substantial sum of money. As soon as the English lawyer had briefed me and told me that there were currently around 2740 claimants to the proceeds of the 51 jewellery trusts, I said, 'No way – it sounds like a snake pit.' No other Indian royal family had this level of indebtedness and financial chaos, and what I had heard about the Nizam himself did not create much confidence. But the lawyer urged me to meet Esra, so I went to see her in her flat in Eaton Square. I thought she was a remarkable woman – upright, straight, clear-headed and trustworthy. So I agreed to help.'

It was Shankardass's amazing achievement to have persuaded all 2740 claimants – legitimate and illegitimate descendants of the different Nizams – to agree to a settlement of the jewel issue, and gradually to whittle down the demands that initially amounted to six times the market value of the jewels to something manageable. It took him and his three junior lawyers nearly four years to cut through what was arguably the biggest and most tangled Gordion knot of litigation in the entire Indian legal system.

In the process he was regularly blackmailed and threatened, both by the Hyderabadi mafia and the claimants themselves. Several turned up armed to his suite and threatened to shoot him; on one occasion he had his car hijacked as he drove to the airport. Once, a claimant who had been disarmed by the hotel staff threatened to throw himself off the balcony unless his demands were met. Shankardass told him to go ahead – and called his bluff. 'There were some extremely rough men among the *sahibzadas* [princes],' he said. 'Undesirable characters – hollow, shallow and proud. I had to have a full-time guard for two years.'

With the backing of all the different claimants, he then had to reach agreement on a sale price with the Indian government who had, at the last moment, banned the export and public auction of the jewels which they rightly regarded as a national treasure. In the end, the government agreed to pay around £40m – less than a quarter of the market value, but much more than anyone had expected the government to offer. Of this, just under half was to go to the Nizam.

Once the jewel money had been sorted out, Shankardass moved on to pay off, or reach some sort of compromise, with the different litigants in the 130-odd legal cases still outstanding against the Nizam. He also settled his remaining debts, then standing at around £3m. Today only three cases still remain unsolved: a dispute with the Indian Income Tax department, an alimony claim involving the Nizam's fifth wife, a former Miss Turkey, and a case against the MLAs of the Hyderabad assembly whose new residential quarters are located on a former courtyard of the Chowmahalla palace and break all the planning regulations the MLAs are themselves elected to preserve.

All this still left a considerable fund for Princess Esra to invest in the restoration and conservation of the Nizam's properties. Esra has the same talent for picking honest and effective people to work for her as her husband once proved to have for employing crooks. To supervise the restoration of Chowmahalla she chose Martand Singh, chairman and one of founders of INTACH, the Indian National Trust for Art and Cultural Heritage: 'The first time I saw the state the palace was in I thought it would be impossible to save,' remembers Singh. 'I really thought it was hopeless – totally unsaveable.'

'It's impossible to say how much had been lost. After the Nizam sacked his 14,000 staff it had just gone to the dogs. Everything that could be was sold off, and the rest was left to rot. Decomposition can set in very quickly in India – one monsoon can do it – and these properties had been neglected for 30 years. It was the worst case of decay I have ever seen. There was so much undergrowth you couldn't see the buildings. There were hundreds of old howdahs and buggies and wheel-less carriages rotting in the corridors and verandahs. The wood was worm-eaten and there was hardly anything left of the Persian carpets or the silk drapes. The lights did not work and many of the chandeliers had all been sold. One of the ceilings had collapsed.

'But when Princess Esra returned and our architect, Rahul Mehrotra, made his initial report, we found that most of the decay was actually cosmetic. The engineering was sound, and despite the rising damp, the roofs were more or less intact. From the first Esra was completely positive. She asked, "How long is this going to take." "Three-four years," she was told. "Too long" she replied. "I want it done in two." And Rahul succeeded – in two and a half.'

The first task was to restore an old service wing of the palace, which was turned into a scholar's retreat, where architects, urban designers, art and ceramic consultants, conservators, specialist carpenters, photographic experts, textile restorers, antique upholsterers, historians and Urdu and Persian scholars could be lodged and fed while they worked on the different collections. A conservation laboratory and museum store area followed. By 2002, the largest team of conservators ever employed on an Indian restoration project were at work, cataloguing, making inventories, and busily restoring the different collections. A group of metal conservators brought in from Lucknow worked with such speed that they managed to restore 20 blades a month. The entire collection of arms, along with the best of the textiles, carriages and photographic records – including the remarkable harem pictures, published here for the first time – were ready for the recent grand opening of the Chowmahalla palace to the public.

Meanwhile, the conservation of the remaining buildings continues. The restoration of the Indo-Saracenic Khilwat Mahal – where state coronations were carried out – is now complete, and today houses the arms and the photographic collections. The restoration of another of the Chowmahalla pavilions – the Afzal Mahal – is currently under way, with a team of Austrian carpenters at work on the doors and woodwork, while other conservators restore the decorative plaster ceilings, moulding and cornices, and renew both the waterproofing and the exterior limewash and stucco. In time, the plan is to use the buildings for concerts, poetic symposia – or *mushairas* – and scholarly conferences, so turning the complex into a cultural centre as well as a museum.

The Nizam's vast archives are still in the process of being catalogued: fifteen Urdu and Persian scholars are currently employed full-time to sift through the material. Already they have stumbled across a major historical discovery: the negotiations which the Nizam conducted throughout the early 1940s with the Portuguese to buy Goa and so provide his state with a port, and with it a real hope – never realised, perhaps thankfully – of remaining independent from India once the British finally quit India.

Last month, Princess Esra returned to Hyderabad from her base on an island off Istanbul, to oversee the progress of her conservation efforts.

She swept in, sari-clad, imperious, a flurry of energy, and as ever, on her arrival everyone stood to attention. Long lines of unframed canvases were laid out along the corridors and she walked past them, giving an instant decision. 'No – not that one. It's Venetian – I don't like it. Not that either. Now look at that – the sixth Nizam out riding with the Kaiser – yes: send that off for restoration immediately.'

Her tour of inspection completed, I asked if, looking back, she had any regrets:

'Many,' she said. 'If I had the head on my shoulders that I have now a few years ago I would never have let things get into the state they did. But I was too young. At the time it all seemed impossible – the law suits, the huge taxes, debts accumulating, criminal cases, people abusing the trust we had put in them. We had no ready cash, and the palaces seemed like white elephants. So we fled, and then terrible things happened. So much just disappeared: jades, miniatures, furniture, chandeliers...'

'And the Nizam?'

'He had a brilliant brain when I met him,' she said. 'He had had the best education money could buy – Harrow, Cambridge, LSE, Sandhurst. But partly because of his diabetes he went into decline, and in the end really, well... disintegrated. Today he keeps to himself in the south of Turkey. Lives very simply – doesn't love extravagance. Lives in a two room flat in Antalya, and spends his time reading and exploring Roman ruins, going swimming in summer... He's upset, of course, that he didn't achieve what he had hoped and he feels awkward that he let so much go. He wishes he had done things differently, but then that is true of most people...'

Now Esra's reserved 47-year old son Azmet hopes to come back to Hyderabad and take on what remains of the family role in the city. Bin Laden and the assorted Islamist extremists who hope to bring back the institution of the Caliphate are no doubt unaware that the man who has the strongest legal claim to inherit the title was until recently a Hollywood-based cameraman who has worked with Steven Spielberg, Richard Attenborough, Nicolas and Roeg and was even responsible for shooting the notorious Sharon Stone starrer, *Basic Instinct.*

'I am planning to spend much more time here,' Azmet told me. 'The death threats and law suits that kept us all away are cleared up now, and I have great affection for this place – I grew up here.'

He paused: 'I am determined to maintain what has been saved. We'll not make the same mistakes again.'

The burqa and the rickshaw

JAVEED ALAM

HYDERABAD is in flux. Unbelievably rapid and far-reaching changes have been taking place in the city over the last few decades. Let me start to unravel these by taking two unusual emblems, both of which I would like to look at as indicators of the 'epic of modernity'. The *burqa* – a veil the Muslim women wear which extends from head to toe and covers the body – is visible across the city. The burqa is ubiquitously present even in the most posh and modern areas of Hyderabad. The *rickshaw* – the tri-wheeler, manually driven and used to commute – has nearly disappeared from the city. It is now rarely seen even in the poorest and most backward areas. The few that are left carry goods. Hyderabad had the largest number of rickshaws compared to any city in India; it was once referred to as the city of rickshaws.

The presence of the burqa in the posh and modern areas and the absence of rickshaws in the poorest and backward areas is somewhat of an incongruity, a departure from the expected, and therefore calls for attention.

How can the burqa be part of the epic of modernity? Well, people have read it, as is the wont, as a rise of conservatism and religiosity among the Muslim community. It may or may not be so; I think it is a bit of both, as in all communities in India. But that is, I presume, the wrong way of looking at the problem. What has actually happened is that the invisible has become visible, all too quickly. *Purdah* – keeping the woman's body from public view – has always been common among conventional Muslim families. Only 30 years ago, education and employment were very uncommon among Muslim women who came from simple, lower middle class backgrounds. Most Muslim women lived their lives in the confines of the home, rarely going beyond the circle of relatives. But the observance of purdah was quite common when in the public domain. Covering oneself with a *chadar* – a long unstitched cloth to cover the face and body – was enough. A sea change is taking place without any fundamental shift in attitudes to the women's body or person. What has been changing is the socio-economic context within which life is being lived.

Those who were *very* poor are still *quite* poor with some degree of marginal upward mobility. But what has rather pronouncedly changed is the life of the lower middle classes. A sizeable section of these groups have seen a noticeable upward movement in income and life opportunities. Education has seen an enormous expansion. And what is unusual is that it has been a trend set by the women. More often Muslim boys have preferred to go abroad, to the oil rich Middle Eastern countries and have bailed their families out of destitution and hardship. There is extra income available for meeting the necessities of life. Women in these families have taken to education in a big way; the girl child is making the best of the opportunities available within the constraints of religious conventions. The emphasis is on technical and job oriented education including the emerging frontier areas of IT education.

What we see as an increase in the visibility of the burqa is actually women out in the public sphere, educating themselves and working in sectors of economy which were completely hidden from their view even 20 years ago. More often, these women credit it to the grace of God (!), the Allah of their faith. They meticulously observe their religion and the burqa is seen as an integral part of their world. How much of it is imposed by the men in the family or reflects their own desire is difficult to say.

Where is the burqa most visible? Around the colleges and educational institutions, IT coaching centres like NIIT, the commercial establishments, offices, and so on. They ride with burqas on their motorbikes and mopeds and fill up the seats reserved for women in the buses. It is not like Saudi Arabia where the women are forced to stay at home, and venture outside only when accompanied by their men. These women are more often alone. They go together to ice-cream parlours and beauty salons and sometimes chat in public places with their boy friends. We know they are Muslim women, but unlike other women we do not know how they look, their faces are hidden but their work is as visible as that of any other women. They inhabit the modern world but modernity, as yet, remains undefined to them. What will happen in the future is uncertain. History will no longer be a guide. I am not sure if this poses a problem; I would rather see it as a challenge to understand the way in which the world is changing.

The story of the disappearance of the rickshaw is far less complicated. In the mid-1970s, auto-rickshaws (three-wheeler, mechanically driven, mini-taxis) made an appearance. Over the next 15 years they slowly replaced the rickshaw. In the 1970s and early 1980s Hyderabad was viewed as a city in decline. There was though a noticeable migration of people to different parts of the world for work. Where one went and for what kind of work varied a great deal in terms of social status and the consequent levels of education. Nevertheless, Andhra Pradesh and Hyderabad in particular contributed a good deal to the making of the Indian diaspora. Among the Muslims, a lot of people from among the lower and lowest middle classes went out, especially to the Middle Eastern countries following the boom generated by petro dollars.

Secondly, in the 1990s, there was a burst of growth in construction activity centred on the building of flyovers, commercial establishments, and multistoried residential complexes, followed by the making of the Hi-tech city. New opportunities opened up for different kinds of work. A couple of factors contributed to the change. With some money coming in from migrant relatives living abroad, and opportunities opening up with the expansion of the city, people shifted to auto-rickshaws, construction work, repair and maintenance, and other such activity. What facilitated this was the slow expansion of education coupled with quotas in employment for Dalits and Other Backward Classes (henceforth OBCs); the poor moved into *adjacent* blue and white-collar jobs. (Of the few rickshaws that have remained, it is the Dalits who have been left behind, plying goods in rickety ones. The rickshaw puller as a group comprised of Dalits, Muslim and some OBCs.)

The disappearance of the rickshaw does not mark the *end of poverty*; it only indicates a relatively pronounced *decline in destitution,* though both are still present in a visible way. It is the story of marginal mobility into adjacent positions requiring higher skill levels. And this, I think, is important in that it is a source of self-esteem and therefore also marks a demand for *recognition* as equals. Ideologies based on egalitarian values informed by community commitments are in the ascendance all over. This, therefore, is also the source of new aspirations.

The priorities in the family have undergone a major change. People now strive for better houses – the old type of hut will no longer do. They want to see their children in schools, to better their lives. The mental horizon of choices is expanding, adding to those margins of freedom where life undergoes re-definitions. This process has been facilitated by the steady working, despite its infirmities, of democracy. The democratic process is opening doors and people are moving out, against all odds, into new spaces where different demands from the world await them. How these are being met are the new biographies being written by ordinary people. Within the successes achieved, tragic endings and mental pathos is also visible all over.

If we put these two developments together, the appearance of the burqa and the disappearance of the rickshaw, a shift of immense consequence lies below, hidden from view, which needs to be drawn out. I would like to suggest here, a little audaciously, that everyday life for the people of Hyderabad has become of central importance. What matters for them most are the rhythms of ordinary, this-worldly life. It is the open side of modernity, unencumbered by universal values, the central importance of the mundane and ordinary in the making of one's happiness.

I am not suggesting that religion has disappeared or become less important. In fact, it is quite to the contrary. It is more visible and, perhaps, matters more today to both Hindus and Muslims. But it does not, and this is the great change, *trump* everyday life as earlier. The simultaneous presence of both, religion and everyday life, and their increasing importance at the same moment, reminds me of a comment Marx made that modernity is the 'contradictions of progress'. And this is what an epic, as a genre, is all about.

It is this story of the contradictions of progress that I want to elaborate. It is also the story of the social progress the people of Hyderabad have made. An overwhelming majority of the people of Hyderabad, as in much of India, live their lives in communities that are still essentially pre-modern in nature. (Modern communities are virtually self-created ones like trade unions or neighbourhood communities or associations of single mothers or ecologists and so on where *exit* is quite easy whereas pre-modern communities are continuous, self-reproducing ones where *exit* is relatively difficult.) These communities, under the simultaneous impact of modernization and the working of democracy, are undergoing dramatic internal changes but without prospects of dissolution as happened in the West under the impact of modernity.

In this context the idea is to write an account that brings to light, first, how different communities have taken to modern life in the last 20 years in contrast to earlier times. I will look at a number of communities but under the generic terms of OBC and Muslim.

Second, I will attempt to draw a picture of the changing relations between these two because of historical animosities, occasionally leading to communal violence. Third, to see the impact of the above on the communal situation, that is, the politics of inter-communal relations.

The OBCs are made up of a large number of communities, mainly among the Hindus (though there is a rare community from among the Muslims who are also included in this category, but let us ignore that for the time being). These are all of low ritual status. Economically, nearly all of them are poor, with low incomes, uncertain employment and possessing simple skills. Most of them were either dependent on other better off social groups or engaged in small self-employed work.

Most of them occupy a shared space, their aspirations intersect, imaginations have similar trajectories, and future expectations are on a common footing. The OBCs both have common organization as well as community specific organizations. Their umbrella organization, the Andhra Pradesh Backward Classes Association, is a federation of community specific organizations. This is indicative both of identification of interests, a shared common space, and differences based on different socio-economic positions occupied by each community. The following are the main communities.

Let us start with the Bhooi, who used to carry the *palki* (palanquin), sell fish, and were employed in the palace of the Nizam in menial positions. The Bhooi(s) were listed as a 'criminal tribe' by the Nizam regime, along with Lambaras and Vadars and some others. Another group with strong community bonds who stick together across all income differentiation are the Loodha. The members of this community used to make and sell *churan* (an indigenous digestive powder), sell arms, and were notorious for extensive dealings in illicit liquor.

The Pardi, another OBC group, are mainly fruit-sellers. They live in close clusters in certain localities, and have strong emotional bonds.

Until about 1952, they were counted among the Scheduled Castes, but were subsequently de-classified.

There is one other important Hindu community in Hyderabad that needs to be referred to. In the old city, the largest social group among Hindus comprises people known as Munoor Kapu. They are different from the Kapu community of coastal Andhra. In the Telangana region they are counted among the OBC.

Then we have the Gowda also known as Kallal, the toddy tappers. They climb up the palm tree with a sling hung around their waist and fix the container at night and go up again in the morning and bring it down with the drink. Within the group, some became more entrepreneurial and collected the entire produce from the area, passing it on to the contractors, and thereby became well off.

Another important group is the milkmen, also known as cowherds. These are comprised of two sub-groups; one is the Goalis and the other the Yadavs. It is said that the former are indigenous to Hyderabad while the latter were migrants from the North. Some of them have taken to agriculture as well. Being enterprising, the migrants have done much better than the Goalis.

There are other backward groups who do not seem to play a significant social or political role, *viz.*, Waddar – stone cutters; Uppara – earth workers, digging wells and tanks; Kurma – a pastoral community, shepherds; Kumara – potters, making earthen utensils; Mangalla, now also called Nai Brahman – the barber or hair dresser; Rajaka – dhobi or washermen, etcetera.

Among the Muslim of Hyderabad no major specific social group of a caste type can be found. There are, however, some small occupational groups which have been included or recommended for inclusion among the OBC. A few of these are Dudekula – cotton de-seeding, i.e., removing seeds from the cotton which is the first stage of the work (probably called Ladaf in North India); Durwesh or Fakir – mendicants who go around singing for purposes of begging; Quereshi – butchers; silver foil makers; bangle makers, etcetera.

Apart from these groups which are oppressed, Muslims, in general, like any other community, are internally differentiated. Muslims live in all parts of Hyderabad but close to 70% of them live in what is called the 'Old' city, which is an extended southern part of the metropolis. Though these areas have seen some development in the last few years, they remain the most backward part of city.

What is also interesting are the housing settlements of some of the Hindu OBCs where a majority of Lodha and Kapu live in close proximity with Muslims. The presence of Bhoi, Gaoli, Pardi is also significant. This is what had earlier made the area communally sensitive and prone to violence.[1]

The OBCs and Muslim do not share a common social space, living a barricaded social existence. There is little social give and take between them. But the important change that has taken place is that violence is now completely shunned and inter-community peace is actively sought and, further, it is being constantly monitored. This is an entirely new feature of social life and politics in the city.

During my field travels in the late 1990s and after 2000, no communal tension of an overt kind was observed, as was the case in the 1980s and early 1990s. At that time one could see rage and murder in the eyes of the people. The fading of memories of violence, which was so endemic at that time, was a pleasant surprise. These memories were becoming more like a remembrance of a historical event. Nor did I find much mention of the violence of those times. A refreshing change obviously seems to be in the making.

This is in sharp contrast to the situation that prevailed in the 1980s and early 1990. It was a period marked by constant small scale rioting, stabbing, looking for revenge; in short, blood letting of all kinds was endemic. All of this culminated in a huge communal conflagration in the winter of 1990-91. This was also the period of

---

1. See my earlier work on Hyderabad, 'Composite Culture and Communal Consciousness: The Ittehadul Muslimeen in Hyderabad' in Vasudha Dalmia and H. von Stietencron (eds.), *Representing Hinduism: The Construction of Religious Traditions and National Identity*, Sage, New Delhi, 1995.

the height of the Babri Masjid-Ramjanma Bhoomi movement and of Advani's *Rath Yatra*. When the Babri Masjid was demolished in December 1992, tension prevailed in Hyderabad, the Muslims were bewildered, but except for a few clashes with the police, there were no riots. The 1990-91 riot was the last major one. The ethnography of violence and rehabilitation was what marked the period then as against one of a process of seeking peace now. There is no concord or sought out consensus. What we have is a tacit understanding that violence will do no good; this is despite the constant efforts of the Sangh Parivar to instigate violence.

The upshot of the mobility among OBCs and Muslim is the ascendance of the stability of this worldly life, in an immediate sense, in the making of one's happiness. Many more people are today living in better houses, eating better and more nutritious food, and wearing quality clothes. There is a new sense of pride in displaying their well-being to others, sending children to private schools (and on top of that, paying for tuition so that they could excel), aspiring to be in professions that command social respect, and so on. What people are seeking is a world of equality, dignity, and self-esteem, which was always beyond their reach. That world is now, many of them think, within their grasp.

To seek revenge now is to, consequentially, mutilate yourself. And nobody wants that to happen. They will continue to support the Majlis or the BJP and VHP, but not at the cost of sacrificing their worldly gains. I doubt if people in large numbers would be prepared to jump into the fray as before. The Majlis is the local body of the Hyderabadi Muslim and it knows the pulse of the people it claims to represent. In association with the clergy, it has appealed to the Muslim not to be provoked when matters develop on an all-India plane in ways which may agitate the hotheads among the community. Similarly, it has worked to diffuse local communal tensions whenever they arise.

The VHP or BJP are different in an important way. They are essentially all-India affiliates of the RSS. Hyderabad is not the sole centre of their activity. They wish to impact politics on an all-India plane. They look at local presence more as an extension of national politics. When this clashes with the compulsions of the local specificity, as often happens in Hyderabad, they do not know what exactly to do and end up calling for a *bandh*. The two protagonists contending for Muslim and Hindu support are not on the same plane of relationship with their presumed constituencies.

Having stated this, one cannot be sanguine about such phenomena as communal violence; large forces are involved with scant regard for popular aspirations of ordinary people. The purpose of my argument is not to suggest an *'impossibility thesis'* about communal riots in Hyderabad. Tension continues to exist and there have been clashes which fortunately were quickly diffused. Provocation also continues to exist. Those who want to polarize the society along communal lines and pit people against one another for political gain have enormous power to manipulate events. The direction of my argument is rather to suggest the *'difficulty thesis'*, which means that unlike in earlier times, it may be far more difficult to use people as fodder in the politics of communal forces. It also suggests that it may now be easier to counsel calm if communal trouble were to erupt somewhere. The difficulty thesis surely holds good for Hyderabad at this juncture.

Shahar baaki hai mohabbat ka nishan baaki hai

JYOTIRMAYA SHARMA

I am a Hyderabadi now. I wasn't born here, nor did I spend any considerable time in this city before I first set foot here on 29 June 2000. My knowledge of the city and its history was negligible and this lack of knowledge did not stretch even to well-worn stereotypes. Charminar was more real as a brand of cigarettes than as an architectural milestone. I only had one friend who hailed from the city, whom I had first met in England, and followed fortuitously to Shimla. He and his family followed me later to Delhi and, finally, I followed him to Hyderabad. I never really forged a mental association between Javeed Alam and Hyderabad, except for the pleasantly quirky way in which he spoke Hindi, and the excellent *bagarey baingan* he and his NRI brother cooked for me in Shimla.

On 29 June 2000, it was love at first sight. Why was it so? The matters of the heart that the heart knows not, or something to that effect is what a French writer had once said. Maybe it was the

* The title of the essay is from Makhdoom Moinuddin's poem 'Bhagmati'. Translated, it means, 'The City remains and so does the symbol of love'.

people, their natural warmth, maybe it was *karma*, and maybe it was a combination of all these things. I still cannot fully explain why this love survives despite many threats to its longevity. But I can now point to a few patterns of explanation and try the impossible, which is to make sense of love in ways that are wordy and rational.

The first reason is that Hyderabad is everything that Delhi is not. I had come here from Delhi, a city I hated and continue to hate for all the right reasons. Delhi too was not my city, but it never even made a feeble attempt to become mine either. It was always for me a port of transition. It reeked of falseness, power and the misplaced flatulence of spiritedness. In sharp contrast, Hyderabad and Hyderabadis were welcoming, gentle, tentative, eccentric, even arbitrary. Its size was what I was used to and felt comfortable about. It had echoes of the cities I have known well: Udaipur, Baroda, Hull, Oxford, Shimla. It was an overgrown village in 2000 pretending hard to be a city. More so, it had a lake in the middle of the city, something that could make anyone born in Udaipur nostalgic, not merely because the lake was *there*, but the sorry state in which it was, the water hyacinth engulfing it periodically. It beckoned to you to come and own it, save it, to have a sense of belonging.

In 2000, I had not come to stay. I had come for a longish period to complete an assignment and had to go back. But I longed to get back, which I did in April 2001. I soon realized that this was the perfect city also to be a writer. It was sufficiently dull and boring in a peculiarly endearing way. It made no excessive demands on you. In the last eight years it has grown, a bit like the water hyacinth in Hussain Sagar, but it still remains its old reasonable self. What greater proof could there be of my Hyderabadi status than the fact that I regularly crib about the traffic, the deteriorating urban infrastructure, say *haao* as a sign of affirmation and argue about the relative merits of Almond House and Pulla Reddy sweets, and when particularly maudlin, map my last journey to the Banjara Hills crematorium, which, incidentally, shall soon go electrical.

The city often reminds me of a few lines Philip Larkin wrote in a poem on Hull, where he describes the city as one where

'Loneliness clarifies. Here silence stands like heat.
Here leaves unnoticed thicken,
Hidden weeds flower, neglected waters quicken,
Luminously-peopled air ascends;
...Here is unfenced existence:
Facing the sun, Untalkative, out of reach.'

This unfenced existence has something to do with Hyderabad's own unique sense of Time. The term '*parson*', literally, day before yesterday or day after tomorrow, becomes in Hyderabad indeterminate time. 'When were you born?' The answer would be, 'abhi *parson*' (just day before yesterday). 'When was the Charminar constructed?' 'Yahi, abhi *parson*' (just, day before yesterday). 'When will you come to repair this gadget?' 'Parson aata hun' (I will come day after tomorrow). The idea of '*parson*' defies characterization of time into definite past, present or future. It gives people a sense of repose, a sense of unhurriedness, and a semblance of peace. The idea of this vast expanse of Time, unfettered by the illusion of permanence or the arrogance of certainty is what gives Hyderabad its confidence to not dwell for too long on the past, not get embroiled in settling scores, imparting to it, as a consequence, the soul of a Sufi.

The inflection in '*parson*' has nothing of the perfidy of the favourite phrase Delhi uses to delay or postpone work and action, which is 'aap chinta mat kariye' (please do not worry). This attitude to Time makes space for people also to commit errors and live with them. It is a city that allows its finest Urdu poet, Makhdoom, to call Stalin (the Russian leader, not Karunanidhi's son) 'humara rehbar Stalin' (our leader Stalin) and still love him. It allows the revolutionary Makhdoom to sing praises of the poet Iqbal as the light of the community as also wax lyrical about Bhagmati as a symbol of love.

I came to Hyderabad at a juncture in life when it becomes increasingly impossible to make new friends. One, at this point, likes to retain the few good ones that are there, consolidate these bonds, and enter middle age in anticipation that middle age would at least last longer than youth and old age will not dawn as rapidly as the teenage years went by. Hyderabad proved me wrong. I have made more friends than I ever did in my entire life. These friends are from all parts of the country as there are those who trace their beginnings to this city. Those from elsewhere do not hanker after returning to a 'promised land' (not even the Bengalis), nor do they indulge in misplaced nostalgia. They live in Hyderabad, belong here and think of the city as the centre of the universe. There is a great element of truth in the often heard phrase, 'Gandipet ka paani piya hai (He/she has drunk the waters of Gandipet Lake). He who drinks these waters stays in Hyderabad forever.

The city has grown since I came here. The IT and biotech boom has brought in people from all over the country. They don't drink water from the Gandipet Lake and, mercifully, will go away in a few years. They live in gated communities, sit in soulless offices, hardly ever mingle with the local community, retire on weekends to the antiseptic but noisy confines of pubs, and return to their pigeonholed existence on Monday morning. They ignore the city and the city ignores them. It neither resents, like Bengaluru does, nor does it pretend to welcome as Gurgaon does with a plastic smile. It casts a cold eye on them, and passes by. The call-centre taxis have attempted to challenge the sense of indeterminate Time, but these are simply seen as a forced alteration in the city's gentle gene by barbarians from the outside.

There have been attempts in recent years to elevate the page 3 culture in Hyderabad to levels comparable to Delhi and Mumbai. The past year has seen the launch of three new 'city magazines', all of them catering to those who make it to the page 3 grade. The only problem with this mission is the numerical lack of celebrities. Despite spirited attempts to convert anyone who is seen at parties more than two times into a page 3 worthy, the experiment remains fledgling. Apart from this, there have been efforts to open the city to modern art other than simulations of Telangana women with parrots on their shoulders, but the beautiful ladies of Banjara and Jubilee Hills still invest in diamonds than M.F. Husain. Diamonds, they know are for ever, while Husain Saheb's heart flutters one day for Madhuri, another day for Tabu, and yet another day for Amrita Rao.

Three obsessions mark Hyderabad's engagement with the world: politics, cinema and all forms of the supernatural. All these are ways of dulling one's senses rather than the other way round, as evident in a neighbouring state. It is a mild quest for oblivion, exploring the realms of nirvana. If this translates into 'sleep', as it does in Lampedusa's *The Leopard*, so be it. We love politicians calling each other names, making asses of themselves and providing uninterrupted entertainment. As if this wasn't enough, cinema drives and moves us. Cinema in all forms. But Hyderabadis rarely get hysterical about their actors and actresses. Doubtless, some of them have a huge following, but I would be surprised if any Hyderabadi would immolate himself if Chiranjeevi or Nagarjuna were to catch a cold or break their big toe.

The stars on earth of the cinematic kind have a hold on Hyderabadis, but they hardly can compete with the celestial ones. Astrology, palmistry, numerology, tarot, and vastu are taken very seriously. When I began looking for a flat to buy in 2001, the properties I looked at fell into three categories. The ones I liked I could not afford, the ones I could afford I did not like, and finally, there were flats which had a kitchen or a bathroom at the entrance. Why? Because vastu dictated it to be so. I had a colleague once who refused to sit on a particular workstation because it was vastu unfriendly. When I expressed my inability to suggest an alternative seating arrangement, she marched in a few hours later with her personal vastu consultant, who suggested a compromise. She had to sit at an angle, something she did till another workstation could be found for her.

Why do I live in Hyderabad? It makes no demands on me by hiding behind labels. The Mumbaikars once spoke of the cosmopolitanism of their city as much as they extolled its distinctive 'character'. Those from Kolkata see their city as a citadel of the cerebral. The categories and the explanations pile up. Hyderabad makes no such claims and yet people belong to it. They extend to it their devotion and it reciprocates in equal measure, in small, subtle and unsuspecting ways.

Sitting with Javed Jabbar, the Pakistani writer and filmmaker, in a restaurant in Hyderabad, the time came of settling the bill. Javed Saheb insisted that he would pay since he was born here, went to school here and that his mother's final resting place was in Hyderabad. The captain of the restaurant heard my argument as well, that of being a current resident and so had privileged rights over someone who had gone away. Having heard both sides of the argument, he gave his decision in my favour: 'Allow him to pay this time since you are our guest, but you can pay next time because you were born here.' The resident 'alien' had won this round.

Recovering the aesthetic

UZRAMMA

Great grandfather Syed Hussain Bilgrami came to Hyderabad from Bilgram near Hardoi in Uttar Pradesh, part of the determined effort of the Nizam Mehbub Ali Pasha and his minister Salar Jung in the later part of the 19th century to build up a competent administration to avoid an Awadh style British takeover. The British were furious. 'Syed Husain is an able young man, but he'll have to go!' noted Wilfred Scawen Blunt in his diary. As it was they had forced the Nizam to cede the cotton-rich lands of Berar. For this he was rewarded with the empty title of Grand Commander of the Bath, or GCB. 'Gave Curzon Berar,' said Mehbub Ali Pasha bitterly.

Family lore says great-grandmother never really took to Hyderabad and always longed for the North Indian air of Bilgram. She was delighted each time Syed Hussain's frankness with his employer angered the Nizam and she was told to pack her bags. This according to family lore was twice, once when he was asked if the Nizam's marriage to two sisters was permissible in Islam, and again when he gave a true report of the people's dissatisfaction. Each time Syed Hussain was requested to return, he did, to his wife's dismay. Some members of that household kept their North Indian language and North Indian village ways, their *Bilgramiyat*, until they died. There was a certain straight-forwardness and outspokenness in contrast to the local or *mulki* tradition of secrecy, double-speak and prevarication. Our family was always considered *ghair mulki,* outsiders to Hyderabad, even sixty years after they settled.

My memories of a Hyderabadi childhood are a series of flashes without beginning or end. I was too young to understand the feverish, *fin-de-siecle* public mood of the last days of the Nizam's rule. My world was the household and the rocky landscape of Banjara Hills. I was used to the comfortable closeness of the women who looked after us in their clean coarse Siddipet sarees. Their clothes were as rough and as satisfying as their food, red rice and spicy *khatti dal*, stronger on the tongue than our refined white table rice and bland nursery dishes. At night we drifted off to sleep with their stories in our ears, stories that went on for days, that looped and turned and had unexpected endings, stories of rajas who cared nothing for riches, animals and trees that gave wise advice, wicked queens and the wisdom of humble people. Of course we were afraid of the dark, it was peopled by *jinns* and *churayls*, witches whose feet faced backwards.

I was everyone's child and no-one's child, loved in a general rather than a particular way, cared for by a grandmother, aunts and older cousins. Mother had lost two babies. Her West Indian gynaecologist who loved her wept when I was born: 'Batul will lose this one too, it's her *kismat*.' But Mamoojan took me to the great homoeopath Baba Jaisurya, Sarojini Naidu's son. I was cured, lived, and thereafter adopted by the entire family. I was shared out among my relatives. My aunts, cousins and carers made up my everyday world. In my early photographs I have a bewildered look. I never knew where I belonged or why I was where I happened to be. A dispersed childhood like mine could only happen in the shelter of the larger family and ours was large, with grandfather's house at its centre. After independence the family began to disperse as uncles took up posts with the Government of India in Delhi and abroad, and my Hyderabad shrank.

Grandfather's house was built above the modest homes of the once-nomadic Banjaras and the graveyard of the Dhers, among the massive billions of years old Deccan rocks, a few miles away from Mehdi Nawaz Jung's Rock House, a shelter for artists and visited by many famous people including Rabindranath Tagore, in which the walls were uncut rocks. My playmate Zohra, the assistant cook's daughter, and I were born a few days and a few yards apart. She and I would straggle down the hill between monsoon showers with tins and scoops to catch grain-sized rainbow swimmers from the rock pools that would dry up in a day or two. Where did the creatures go when the pools dried up? Do they still exist or are they extinct, perhaps never known to science, never having had a name? I don't see any rock pools around Banjara Hills now, because all around Hyderabad the rocks themselves are almost all gone, blasted to bits, except where old shrines perch at their summits.

My cousins and I were expert rock jumpers, creeping out in the afternoon sun while the grownups slept. We knew exactly where to place our feet on the huge sloping sides to reach the heights. The empty rockscape was magical, particularly in the monsoons. Strange curly green leaves would appear close to the ground, tiny flowering plants and the red velvety *birbahutis* that would emerge after the first showers, creatures that would curl up into little cushions when we touched them. In the rains millipedes invaded the house. Scorpions lurked under carpets and snakes in water pipes. Bigger fry too, including panthers, prowled Banjara Hills all year round, picking up our chickens and pet dogs even as late as forty years ago.

The land belonged to no one; it had little or no monetary value. Once the Golla shepherds wandered freely over it with their flocks. Now it is all enclosed, private property, transformed into real estate, and we can no longer walk all the way to Golconda Fort as we used to, following the secret channel that supplied the fort with water 500 years ago.

We flew kites during Sankranthi, the kite festival. For long I believed, incorrectly as it turns out, that it was only in Hyderabad that the upper part of the kite string is coated with ground glass, the better to cut down the opponents' kite in kite wars. We threw stones at unripe mangoes to bring them down, picked green tamarind with hooked sticks and shook down *jamuns* and those curly bean-like fruit that grew wild on the trees in no-man's land. There were experts among us who could spin heavy wooden tops, carefully winding them with thick cotton string before flicking them into motion. *Chirki billa, lone paat* didn't need any equipment, only flat stones and lines drawn on the ground. In summer we ate crushed ice balls dipped in coloured syrups, in winter roasted palm roots and spiced *chana*, and all year round the bright pink strands of sugar that were called *buddi ke baal* – all bought from street vendors and strictly forbidden by parents.

The Hyderabad cousins went to day schools, one of the three that were part of the Anglicized education system: the Mahbubia School for girls, the Hyderabad Public School and St. George's Grammar, and during my long visits to Hyderabad I went with them. There was a public bus each morning – number 127 – which, by the way still runs. At one of the stops, if the children were not ready, the bus would wait, and a cup of tea would be sent out for the driver.

Why were we sent to these schools, and why did our parents, so well read themselves in Farsi and Urdu, not pass on their learning to us? I was deposited at the age of eight in a boarding school run by English ladies mainly for the children of English tea planters, and there I stayed till I was 16, reading Wordsworth and Shelley rather than Ghalib and Mir. Most of the cousins and their friends were subjected to this Anglicization, which made us as Ananda Coomaraswamy says 'strangers in our own land'. Still, the folk culture that cocooned my childhood was never quite wiped from my memory, remaining buried in the lower depths, only to surface years later when I came back to Hyderabad in middle age.

But though I didn't know it, the seeds of fundamental change had taken root in my own small but influential circle: we had taken too well and too early to Anglicization. When Curzon came to Hyderabad it was great-grandfather who could converse with him in his own language. Four generations later this eclecticism turned against itself and produced me, a product of a perfectly English boarding school education, knowing nothing of the Urdu and Farsi in which my parents had played *antaakshri*.[1]

Hyderabad's rocks extend through the Deccan plateau and with it the Dakhni language, though both are now at the edge of extinction. There is a softness to the culture, made up of multiple strands and a shading from one strand to another; to call it a synthesis of 'Hindu and Muslim' is to simplify it for the modern westernized mind that confuses complexity with chaos. The shrines and the *bastis* have defied the divisions that the fundamentalists try to create. From my window Guruji and I watched during the 'communal riots' of 1992, the basti dwellers were determined to resist the mischief of setting one against another. Hindus and Muslims together formed vigilant groups to keep watch at night, and turned back the invasions. This happened in bastis all over the city.

I came back to Hyderabad when in my middle age, this time for good. For years I had longed to settle in one place. I had moved in my childhood every three years, to Father's railway postings in the small railway towns of North India, in later married life too. Hyderabad though was the constant home but with unexplored dimensions. Bewildered as a child, I was ignorant as an adult of my cultural heritage, language, and the world around Hyderabad. Dakhni Urdu was my mother tongue but had receded to inaccessibility until in my middle age I met Ravinder Sharma, Guruji of Kala Ashram, who gave it back to me. The Hyderabad of the last years of the 20th century gave me the first real chance to be myself. I learnt the sweet Telugu of Telengana too, known until then only through a nursery rhyme about broken swings.

1. A verbal game still common throughout India, in which competing teams have to come up with poems, rhymes or today, songs from films beginning with the last letter of the rhyme quoted by the opposing team.

Conversation with Guruji recalled my everyday Dakhni, and I discovered from Father's repertoire the Dakhni verse of Mohammad Quli Qutb Shah:

Piya bin pyala piya jai na
Piya bin ekthil jiya jai na
Kathe hain piya bin suburi karun
Kaha jai amma kiya jai na.[2]

When I returned I set out to investigate the roots and branches of craft as expression of the makers. It was the first step in my exploration of local folk traditions and folk culture that would in my mind open the door to a different way of organizing society. I travelled in the villages around Hyderabad and discovered the world of the artisans, the weavers, metal smiths and wood carvers and turners. My bewilderment with life finally disappeared. The first long hot summer of my return I sat in the libraries of the Gazetteers' Office and the Archaeology Museum and read all that I could find on textiles and natural dyeing. It seemed important to catch the essence of a way of being that was being lost in the surge towards an alien modernity.

By now the thick strong cotton Siddipet sarees that used to be woven specifically for the Golla community had lost their weight and bulk and become featureless. Other crafts and textiles too had been forced into gentrification, the *telia rumal* no longer worn as head cloth by Malas and Madigas, but translated into sarees for city women, losing its thickness like the Siddipet sarees. Of course the *nakashis* of Nirmal no longer made their own paints. There were still a few calligraphers in the city, others like the *kagzis*, makers of fine handmade paper, had given up altogether. The bangles sold in Lad Bazaar are no longer made in the lanes behind it, but are imported from Jaipur, and now who knows? Perhaps even China.

Use and aesthetic are the warp and weft of a material object. What happened to the Siddipet saree and the telia rumal seems to

2. 'Without the beloved I cannot taste the cup,/ Without the beloved I cannot live even a moment; / They say I should endure the absence of the beloved: / ...easy to say, but impossible to do.'

provide a clue to the change that has come about in the material culture of the city. The outward form is preserved while its essential quality and use value are lost. The yarn of the telia rumal was oiled for a practical purpose: it kept the heads of Malas and fishermen who worked long hours in the sun cool, while the sturdy cotton sarees woven for the women of the Golla community withstood the rigours of their working lives.

If someone were to ask me what has changed in Hyderabad between my childhood and middle age, it would not be the physical changes that would first come to mind – the transformation of a unique Deccan landscape with its two-and-a-half billion year rock clusters and architecture of its time and place into an anonymous city of the Third World. Nor would it be the proliferation of malls, gated communities and high rises. Today those transformations are spoken of with pride: An advertisement for a 'dream project' boasts 'Heavy machinery crush [sic] boulders to minute particles…' Jinns and *churayls* have nowhere to hide now, the nights are bright with electric lights and noisy with television and traffic. Ancient trees and heritage buildings are mercilessly sacrificed to road-widening or gigantic shopping malls. The 500 year old Hussain Sagar is constricted to a fraction of its original size, the many other city lakes that kept Hyderabad cool in summer are built over. It would not even be the loss of the aesthetic, the thoroughfares dotted with Donald Duck waste bins and huge billboards.

These are only the outward signs of what has changed. A child growing up when I did in the Hyderabad of the 1940s and '50s was a little speck in a warm cultural soup. It was not a paradise for all, far from. It was a feudal polity with large disparities between rich and poor, but it allowed its many distinct *jatis* and peoples to be themselves, to practice their traditions and rituals in their own ways. There were areas in which everyone could share and be equal – in the games which did not need costly equipment, the kite flying, the street food. The sharing made for a gentleness in the cultural mix that was the hallmark of Hyderabad, and the essence of its character.

I don't believe that the changes have happened as an inevitable outcome of modernity. The power to direct change has always been in a few hands and so it remains, though the hands themselves are now different. The new rulers do not sit at the feet of their own wise men and women or of the humble folk, as the kings did in the old stories; they prefer the advice of aliens from a very different culture. That culture comes from countries of ice and snow and struggle against nature. It does not suit our soft climate where we work with nature, not against it... or we used to. Now the forests that channelled the huge monsoon rains gently into the earth are gone, so we suffer floods. Rivers are dammed so that the craft industries on their banks decline. 'But the Sun has continued to give forth to India its vast vivifying rays, the Heavens to pour down upon the vast surface its tropical rains,' as Francis Carnac Brown, a cotton planter of the 19th century says. Nature, desecrated and desacralized though it is, is still the *annadata*.[3] Custard apple, mango, tamarind, soapnut trees spring up of themselves; stick a branch of *sejni* in the stony soil and it fruits within the year.

The quintessential Hyderabad is still there too, just below the surface, waiting for the infatuation with so-called modernity to recede. It's there in the shrines and bastis which the different faiths share. The legendary hospitality of Hyderabad can still be found; a stranger is still offered water, tea, even a meal in the poorer parts of the city if not in posh Banjara Hills. You can still sit for hours in an Irani *chai khana* over a 'one-by-two', a cup of tea halved between two friends. The guardians of Hyderabadi-ness are the ordinary people – Lambadas, Dhers, village or city Muslims with folk traditions that horrify the purists, craftspeople, people who are secure enough in their own multi-layered heritage to share with others, who have not re-defined themselves out of fear into a single dimension. They keep their Hyderabadi grace.

---

3. *Annadata*: sustainer, literally food-giver.

A life less ordinary

FEROZE GUJRAL

HAVING mostly lived abroad, India to me has always meant Hyderabad. Hyderabad in the hot flush of summer, sparkling at festivals, decked in all its finery at marriages and deep indigo in death.

My first memory of Hyderabad was probably a mixture of fragrances – the exotic aroma of jasmine put under every pillow in the house at dusk, the heavy musk of insect-repelling incense being taken from room to room as the maid recited verses of the Koran, the bitter smell of neem leaves being boiled for our bath, the scent of wild Indian rose from my eldest grandmother and French perfume from the youngest, but most sharply, the fragrant sandalwood in my hair.

All other memories appear and disappear against the backdrop of our ancestral great house 'Khan Balik', named after the summer home of the great Genghis Khan. The house sat in a compound of five houses – one in the centre that belonged to my great grandfather and the other four smaller ones built for his four wives. By the time I was born, the government had already appropriated three houses, and the last two would revert at the passing away of both my great grand uncle and my grandfather.

Numerous bedrooms, long winding corridors, cool marble floors, multi-shuttered windows, high ceilings, and a perpetual hum of muted conversation, faint music and laughter trickling though the lattice ventilators disturbed only by the call to prayer five times a day. Corridors lined with coloured hanging pumpkin lights, rooms decorated with animal skins and trophies, large priceless Ming vases, and books from all over the world held court. Drawers laden with silver wear and Venetian mirrors with painted scenes and finely cracked Wedgwood plates mirrored our every expression.

Belgian crystal chandeliers and doorknobs all coated with *attars* that wafted on the hems of rustling fabric hiding jewelled feet. Last but not the least, the tragically beautiful derelict tapestry fans that fluttered in mute mortification by the wind of its more modern version. All these had their esteemed place, as did the humans in this grand house and specially me, the first great grandchild. It was like living in a jewel box; textures vied with colours and fought failing battles with gloss and shine.

Since most of the elders observed *purdah*, all traders came to the back entrance of the house – from vegetable sellers to silk merchants, from the dhobi to the jewellers and the pundits. My grandfather, a six foot six Pathan, was also known as *panch seri nawab*. This signified his capacity to consume five sers of rice in one sitting. This rice of course was especially sent from a particular rice field somewhere in Pakistan famed for its outstanding and rare fragrance. These sacks always arrived with the insignia of the chrysanthemum throne of Japan and our family name printed below it. This was the only paddy field that the Japanese royal family got their rice from for hundreds of years. Honeydew melons came from Afghanistan, pistachios from Iran, dates from Iraq and opium from Tashkent. The other precious foods were saffron from the crocus flower of the Kashmir highlands and morel mushrooms from Lahore.

The traditions of the house were wide and varied. From different wives and cars to different areas for males and females, we also had different kitchens for vegetarian and non-vegetarian food and needless to say different cooks, most important of whom was the one who made sweetmeats. Abdul Rehman had my grandfather's ear and was the most powerful and most feared of all the three dozen odd domestics. He had a sorcerer's talent at lacing any dessert or sweet with aphrodisiacal, gripe-inducing, hallucinatory or poisonous ingredients; he was my favourite of all the domestics and from him came my pet name of Begum Para.

The car sheds at the rear of the compound had a line-up of cars of all shapes and sizes. Most of them, however, never ever functioned. Half of those that did remained in purdah. The clearest memory I have is of all us cousins and aunts piled-in to see the annual all-India exhibition. These trips were of supreme importance to my young aunts who spent sleepless nights thinking about what they would wear, how messages to their potential love interests would be sent and finally how they would get the seat by the window in the car so as to allow for the edge of their *dupatta* to show so the concerned individual could spot the car his lady love was in. Bribery and corruption was rampant in our little worlds as we did favours, watched doors and stole the old heavy black phones and crawled from room to room on all fours to avoid detection.

Shaded from the harsh summer sun, the *khus*-lined coolers tempered the days that were passed in strange pursuits peculiar only to Hyderabad. Competitions held for eating the maximum number of mangos and raw tamarind left our tongues softened with mango pulp and cut with tamarind while hide-and-seek exposed more and hid less than most of the adults would have liked. We girls were taught exotic braiding of the hair, home remedies for beautifying ourselves and wily recipes to find everlasting love. Rearranging my grandmother's jewellery drawers according to the colour of the gems while trying on each piece brought such delicious delight as did dressing up as Anarkali and reading dog-eared comics borrowed from second-hand libraries. Lessons in Urdu and casual history and readings of the great

Sufis guaranteed the gentle drugging of all the children to deep sleep every noon.

The cool Deccan nights were spent on the expansive roof of the house. Beds were lined with mosquito netting and maids went from person to person gently washing feet in ceramic basins and placing them on the beds while the elders gave lessons in astronomy and stars were charted with pudgy fingers held lovingly in gnarled hands. Ghost stories that grew more horrific and unbelievable each year were finally related in whispers as we fell asleep, only to be carried down at dawn, softly drenched in dew.

Once a year, however, we would shift *en masse* into the catacombs under the Qutb Shahi tombs. Tented structures, carpets, beddings and hoards of utensils were transported, including dressing tables, gramophones and radios. Adults spent all day at *shikar* in the surrounding wilderness, as we slid into the magic spell of the tombs enveloped by moonlight and music and spent till midnight chasing ghostly myths amongst the ruins. Many a great love story began here without the traditional segregations of the house. The other important trip was made to the small town of Vikarabad, given in dowry to my great grandmother. My mother was named Viqar after it. The word means 'dawn', and it is here that our ancestral tombs still exist.

All rites and rituals were strictly adhered to in my grandfather's house – shaving the head on the 40th day, tasting the first grain, piercing the ears, initiations into learning the holy script, celebrating my coming of age and finally marriage at age 17 were all done in grand Islamic style. My grandmother's *takhat posh*, the *khada dupatta* in our family colours, flower jewellery, *henna* designs spun with needle and thread, bathing in turmeric milk and rose water, blessing of 21 goats for charity and being weighed in silver all enfolded amidst the singing of *gazals* and *qawalli*, the recitation of *sher shairi*, and readings from the Koran – all presided over by three grandmothers made my marriage unforgettable.

Weddings were almost two weeklong affairs; my great aunt Asima's being the most elaborate. The invitation cards were of pure silver cloth woven with her name in real gold, all desserts had gold leaf and *paans* had crushed pearls in them. Her wedding lasted 11 days and nights.

Asima Begum was an innocent beauty with an iron willed heart. She rejected all proposals on the excuse that the man in question had never made an effort to get to know her or romance her as she deserved, i.e. celluloid style. She finally married a man who not only charmed her by sending 365 outfits with matching shoes and jewellery in 365 shades of colour, but also discovered and accepted her secret habit of smoking by sending her an exquisite Cartier cigarette holder. Needless to say we all fell in love with him too.

Our birthdays were marked by the tying of a pearl in a knot to a silken skein of coloured thread that hung in my grandfather's almirah. My colour was turquoise blue befitting my name. My first birthday cake contained grey Basra pearls and I was weighed in gold, which was given in charity. The most fun was at festival times when if you didn't wake early enough and get to the dyer first to choose your own unique colour combination, you could end up at Eid dinner drably dressed in a colour so dark and grey that you could be deemed to be in mourning. Eid dinners were set on the rooftop laid out with low *divans* and banquet style placements. Tall mirrors were placed along one side of the setting so as to allow both sides to enjoy the pleasure of sighting the moon. I spent most of such evenings peering at the mirrors trying to spot other cousins and the possibility of seeing some adult beauty in myself.

My great great grandfather had four wives, two of whom bore girl children that did not survive. On the insistence of a Hindu pundit, the next girl child was given a male name and the child survived. Henceforth, for many generations we have followed this tradition; my daughter being the 5th generation named Alaiia after my Turkish great grandmother's family. My grandfather also married twice. His second wife who was English was my grandmother. A beautiful and tall Oxford educated redhead who while converting to Islam and remaining in purdah for many of her early years in Hyderabad, nevertheless insisted on keeping pets, a completely forbidden thing to do. Her endless and peculiar entourage, however, made our vacations unforgettable – Pepo the wicked monkey, Sammy the black cat, Leo the leopard, the croaking cockatoo, the two all white German Shepherds, Snowy and Whitey, and two snakes that spent most of their time knotted to a curtain rod.

On each visit one was morphed into the wondrous old ways of the house. Speech became flowery like the beautiful Urdu spoken, idioms and couplets spilled from the tongue like sweet nectar, and an overriding desire to be dressed as an archaic Mughal princess persisted for days after one had left.

Our childhood, I realize only now, was played out during the last dying moments of a grand old city of great historical importance and Islamic culture. The Mughals, the Qutb Shahis and the great Nizams had with their immense wealth, culture and excesses put Hyderabad on the world map for all time. From the glittering *galis* of Lad Bazaar to Van Cleep and Arpel in Paris and the crystal makers in Belgium, my grandparents commanded both respect and awe because they were from Hyderabad, land of the Nizam. Once the richest man in the world, who's famed 150 wives were well known by jewellers and craftsmen in Europe both big and small. It was the land of the famous Golconda diamonds, land of exquisite language, cuisine, music, homes, and immense style.

To me Hyderabad will always signify a Muslim way of life seen nowhere else in India. Today there exist none of the great houses or the families, or the culture that once signified the Hyderabad way. All that remains alas of this lost culture and precious world is my velvet-lined drawers of forgotten jewels, my name, a family tree from the 1300s and my memories of a life less ordinary.

A story of sartorial amalgamation

RITU KUMAR

FROM ancient times, the Deccan and the region around has produced the finest of cotton and embellished it with the deft use of vegetable dyes to create dramatic, artistic patterned fabrics. Exported from India in dhows to the Middle East and Europe, the fabrics and patterns set a 'fashion fever' for Indian chintzes. Here in India, the many kingdoms patronized the craft and used the fine skills of the master weavers and printers as well as the fine expertise of those who embellished the textiles.

The Greek historian, Herodotus, marvelled at the quality of Indian cotton, noting, 'There are trees which grow wild, the fruit of which is a wool exceeding in beauty and goodness than that of sheep. The Indians make their clothes of this tree wool.' This reference is to the great cotton-weaving belt of India stretching from the present Tamil Nadu to Andhra Pradesh and Gujarat. Records suggest that the most sophisticated of the Deccan cottons were printed and dyed, whereas others were patterned on the loom with gold, silver, cotton and silk threads.

The Indian courts prized these stunning fabrics, commonly referred to in poetic terms such as the 'flower cloth' or *pushpapatta*, and the 'picture muslin' or *chitra virali*. However, these historical facts tell us little about how the fabrics were used or fashioned; nor do we get any clues about the styles in which the men and women of that ancient period dressed. Were their ensembles fashioned in a way that was more sophisticated than what we see on the ramp today?

In ancient India, women wore unstitched garments called *kayabandhan* and *antariya* – much like a small sarong, held up with a chunni-like sash at the waist, their hair dressed in formal fashion with enviable variations in style. Women through the medieval period, especially in the Deccan, favoured more or less the same ensemble. The rest of the ensemble consisted of little else barring the elaborate jewellery that adorned every part of the body and hair. The torso was not covered except with dramatic neckpieces that emphasised the breasts. Male attire was similar, with equally elaborate jewellery and formal coiffure.

A 5th century Ajanta painting gives us the equivalent of India's first *Vogue* cover. It shows sophisticated stitched attire accessorised with some unstitched scarves. In contrast to images of women of ancient India, in this medieval figure the breasts are covered. The figure is of an exotic dancing girl dressed in a tight-fitting tunic. The back is cut high and the breasts are fitted with a white choli. The sleeves are made of a dotted fabric which appears to be tied and dyed in the *bandini* technique. The front panel of the blouse narrows at the waist leaving most of the midriff bare and hangs loose over a fitted sarong made out of what seems to be a sophisticated *ikat* fabric. The hair is dressed in three tiers and decorated with what looks like carved white flowers. The jewellery consists of necklaces, earrings, bracelets, a crown and hairpins.

For sheer drama, mystery and an avant-garde sense of fashion, this image is my favourite fashion muse – it transgresses time, and is as much in fashion today as it was in the Gupta period. There is not much to report on Hindu women's clothing through the ages till the advent of the British Raj. Fashion sense remained tenacious as Indian women continued with, and do till today, their preference for wearing unstitched garments though the draping styles of the sari and the odhni went through many variations.

Stitched garments included cholis, lehngas or ghaghras and the shalwar with a tunic in endless variations. Men's fashion too underwent a change in medieval India. Records show the inclusion of the transparent white *angrakha* worn over the pyjama, with elaborate headgear and jewellery, albeit used more judiciously than in ancient India. Thereafter, men's fashions did not remain as resilient as those of the women since the dress rules changed with the advent of the Muslim court. The identity of Hindu noblemen was established by the style of turbans they wore, while the rest of the attire was based on the prescribed norm in the particular court. Subsequently British rule introduced the three-piece suit that was worn with these turbans through the 19th century.

In the 12th and 13th centuries Muslim rulers, primarily the Turkish speaking ones from Iran, Central Asia and Afghanistan, conquered most of northern India and established a culture that was closely linked to the civilization of the eastern Islamic world. Ruling from Delhi, they infiltrated southwards in the early 14th century, finally subduing the Deccan, which until then had been ruled by Hindu kings. In 1347, a Muslim officer serving in the Deccan rebelled against the Sultan of Delhi, assumed the title of Bahman Shah, after the legendary hero of the *Shahnama*, and founded the independent Bahmanid dynasty. His huge empire stretched across the south of the Vindhya mountains, from the Arabian Sea to the Bay of Bengal. In the 15th century, provincial governors established five Deccani sultanates. The great developments in art and culture happened in these three kingdoms – Ahmadnagar, Bijapur and Golconda. Islamic rule was to prevail for the next six centuries, until 1950 when the last Nizam of Hyderabad relinquished power.

A surprisingly large proportion of fashion masterpieces were produced for the mysterious sultans of the Deccan in the plateau of southern India during the 16th to the 17th centuries. Unfortunately, no actual garment has survived the hot humidity of the Deccan. This makes for a frustrating situation, a reality that disallows study of the elaborate garments because it is important to feel and touch the fabrics, see the detailing of stitching and the intricate finishing that spells sophistication and skill.

When I was writing my book *Costumes and Textiles of Royal India,* I realized that in India most historical information comes to us through secondary sources, and history writing is often left to the mercy of conjecture. At the risk of taking some liberties and stating my conclusions from the wealth of Deccan paintings that are sprinkled across museums in the UK and Germany, I will share with you my take on the Muslim fashions of the Deccan region.

Little research has been done on the Deccani kingdoms themselves and less so on the textiles and fashions they produced. The three kingdoms of Bijapur, Golconda and Ahmadnagar patronised the painting of cloth because of strong cultural links with the Middle East, especially Safavid Iran. Though Deccani fashions have long been confused with Persian, Turkish or Mughal court art, a study of the costumes worn in Deccani paintings immediately establishes their provenance, as the clothing worn in the paintings displays its unique character.

Owing as much to lush sensuality of South Indian fabrics as to the Persian traditions of style and dress codes, I suspect that the fashions were influenced by two factors. First, the suitability of cotton in the hot climate necessitated a change in the drape and structure of the coats and heavy garments worn in Turkey. Hence the use of the jama, often in the indigenous angarakha style (angarakha is a term which loosely translated could mean *anga rakshak* in Sanskrit, or the protector of the body). This crossover style of the *jama* is seen worn by the male nobility of the Deccan and in the *chakdar jama* with its many *avatars*. These lightweight coats seen on royal personages, are styled with the Mughal patkas, the silk sashes worn at the waist, and Turkish turbans.

The second and more visible influence seems to be that of the *kalamkari* painter and printer. It was this influence that compelled the fashion of the Deccan court to divert from the sparse *butis*, floral and other motifs of the Mughal courts, and the geometrics of the Jaipur printing school. The patterning on the garments is dense; the compositions are reflective of the local flora and fauna and there is an exuberant use of floral *jaals* with intense colours creating a lyrical, albeit rustic, romanticism.

This genre of clothing developed an unique indigenous character, alien to both the sobriety of the Mughal court and to the calligraphic subtleties of the Iranian court, reflecting the indigenizing of the Shahs. As the splendour of the Golconda and Bijapur Empire grew, so did the studied formality of court costumes. Baroque in nature, they were to set a different 'handwriting', rarely written or even discussed in fashion terms. The layering of garments and mixture of colours and designs is typical of the Deccan kingdoms in the late medieval period intended to enhance a sense of opulence.

Descriptions from my book will give the reader a sense of what these Sultans really looked like – 'The Sultan Abu'l Hasan Tana, Shah of Golconda wearing a richly patterned jama with rouched sleeves, a three-quarter sleeved *farji* or coat with bold, floral motifs and a sumptuous golden shawl, a delicately ornamented patka and a striped *chouridar pyjama*. Although the patterns of the clothing are a blend of Persian and Indian styles, the pointed collar of his jacket and the ermine wrap are very Central Asian. An attendant holding the patterned umbrella, wearing a white jama and dhoti contrasted against all the patterning, is a relief.'

The women of the Deccan wore costumes that established the religion they practiced. By this point in time, the acceptance of *purdah* was a way of life for the royal and aristocratic families of the Shahs, as well as in the courts. It had come to be symbolic of the strict adherence to Islam. Deccani paintings unfortunately, give no evidence of women in the harems. Interestingly, when women are portrayed in the paintings they seem to be Hindu women dressed in exotic sarees and cholis.

There is a wonderful panel from 17th century Pulicat (Madras region), showing three women in motion, wearing ghaghras or gathered skirts and odhnis or long scarves with short half-sleeved cholis or bounces. The bold patterning and colours of their garments is typical of the Deccan style. Their hair is neatly dressed and two of the women have long tasselled braids. Almost as an ominous warning, the panel on the side shows Europeans, probably traders, dressed in tights and short jackets with ruffled collars.

As for the Muslim women, I have to conjecture again. The way the women of the harem dressed would have been dictated by their luxurious surroundings and languorous lifestyles, which revolved around bathing, grooming and dressing. Originally the clothes worn by Muslim women were not dramatically different from those of the men, and were in marked contrast to the sensuous clothing which had long been favoured by high-ranking women of the Hindu courts. They perhaps wore long, loose jama-like robes, which had full sleeves and opened at the front. Underneath that was worn an ankle-length vest, pyjamas, voluminous and exotic, styled to be worn under the entire ensemble, that was complete with a veil that covered most of the hairstyle and face. There was little display of the body and preference was given to layered clothing.

Though outside the harem they wore the burqa, I presume that with the intermingling of cultures and races from across the world within the harem, the style mix was eclectic. There must have been a diverse selection, an obvious shift towards greater sensuality, which was the combined result of the influence of Hindu fashions, the climate and the relaxed lifestyle of the harem. Love for gold ornamentation, *zardozi* embroidery, kalamkari floral fabrics, ikats and the Bengal and Lucknow embroidery, tone on tone, has been recorded, but I only wish we had been left with at least some garments of this genre.

The men's dress and gear could certainly have made for the grand finale of a great fashion show anywhere in the world. I quote, 'There was a certain style of wearing the farshi or pyjama that evolved in the Muslim courts. The gote train was artfully folded by a maid and held by the wearer in her left hand, leaving the right free. The pallav of the odhni was draped so long that it almost touched the floor... The ensemble had such royal grace and elegance that you did not just walk into a room, you made a dramatic entrance.'

With the coming of the British, there was a gradual but inevitable shift toward western styles. Silhouettes were streamlined as the garments became more fitted – hence the appearance of fitted coats like the bandgala, achkan and *sherwani* – standard indigenous formal attire in 20th century India. Achkans were often worn with a white collar following European fashion, over a pair of trousers or a dhoti and with an assortment of accessories. The result was a mixture of styles, some elegant and some gauche.

The increased interaction with the British saw most women from royal families come out of purdah in the 1900s. This necessitated a change of dress. Indira Devi of Cooch Behar popularised the chiffon saree. She was widowed early in life and followed the convention of abandoning her richly woven Baroda shalus in favour of the traditional unadorned white. Characteristically, she transformed her 'mourning' clothes into high fashion. She had sarees woven in France to her personal specifications, in white chiffon, and introduced the silk chiffon saree to the royal fashion repertoire. The chiffon saree did what years of fashion interaction had not done in India. It homogenised fashion across this land. Its softness, lightness and beautiful, elegant, caressing drape was ideally suited to the Indian climate.

Different courts adopted their own styles of draping and indigenizing the saree. In most of the courts the saree was embellished with stitching hand-woven borders in gold from Varanasi, delicate zardozi work, *gota*, *makaish* and *tilla* work that embellished the plain fabric, sumiltaneously satisfying both traditional demands and ingrained love for ornamentation. Some images of maharanis in the Deccan show the women wearing a sleeveless, richly embellished waistcoat over their blouses. The Begum of Savanur remembers how sumptuous the chiffon saree became at their gatherings. At some courts it was worn with jaali, or net kurtas and embossed silk waist length *sadris* or jackets. Some of them were so rich that the entire ground was embroidered over with pearls and zardozi.

Princess Niloufer from Hyderabad was among the last of the Imperial Ottoman princesses. In 1931, at the age of 15, she was married to Prince Mauzzam Jah, the second son of the Nizam of Hyderabad, one of the richest rulers in India. Her clothing collection took on a more European style with Mlle Fernande Cecire designing her sarees. The designer gave a glamorous, asymmetrical pattern of sequins which covered one shoulder and the pleats. The collection was bequeathed, after her death, to the National Institute of Fashion Technology in Delhi.

Post-independence, fashion trends from across the country continued to become homogenous, insufficiently cognizant of the fact that sartorial tastes are both ingrained in the country and dependent largely on the craft and textile culture of this rich and diverse land. Unfortunately, the contribution of the Deccan has not been sufficiently recorded. It gave Indian fashion its first amalgamation of a true blend of Ottoman tastes with the craft of the kalamkari, embellished and enriched with a large dose of ikat from the region, further ornamented with zardozi and thread embroidery. The over-the-top garments with this mixture of fabrics and techniques made a fashion statement worthy of an exuberant finale anywhere in the world.

Hyderabadi tales

VANAJA BANAGIRI

EVOLUTION has found a new destination – Hyderabad. Or should that be revolution? Any which way you look at it, whatever term you wish to use to describe the winds of change that have swept the city, one thing is certain: Hyderabad has arrived. And how!

Gone are the days of *nawabi* attitudes and laid-back lifestyles. Everything is on a fast track. From economic development to attitudinal change, Hyderabad has undergone a tremendous metamorphosis. Steering the growth are the city's young. With their restlessness to be a part of the hip and happening, and energy levels to match, they have redefined all things hitherto known as Hyderabadi.

Shopping, clubbing or weddings – every single opportunity is an event to be celebrated. Larger than life. A 20 something doesn't bat an eyelid before she picks up Jimmy Choo shoes or a Prada bag. And the big fat middle-aged Hyderabadi has turned into a six-pack exhibitionist strutting his stuff. Male manicures are a daily norm and tequila shots nightly rituals. While the rest of the country parties on weekends, Hyderabadis do it every day. Eves nights at night clubs and pubs are jam-packed with the young and the not so old, while the fuddy-duddies are having a whale of a time in their Jubilee Hills, Banajara Hills mansions.

With all that shopping and endless partying, one would assume career and education come secondary. No siree, that's where you're mistaken. From a 26-year-old businessman to a 23-year-old practicing lawyer, they're all focused about what they want, how to get it and where to go from here. Focus is the latest open sesame. A 22-year-old salsa instructor who earns more than her doctor parents did at her age for teaching the city's swish set 'the moves', gives a piece of sound advice to her 50 year old dad: 'What's most important is to know what you want from life and focus on how to get it. Mine is earning mega bucks so that I can travel in style.' New age 'you can make it happen' self-help writers could take a leaf out of her *mantra*, eh? Looks like.

While material pleasures rule the lives of 80% of the young, the rest have already gone the whole hog of spiritual shopping. 'I have been through "art of living", transcendental meditation, reiki, alpha mind power workshops.' 40-year-old woman facing mid-life crisis? Nah. It's Nisha, a promising interior designer who believes that there is a need to practise 'detached attachment'. So is she dedicating her life to spirituality? 'That's where most people lose it. Spirituality is not divorced from everyday life. We all need to focus.' Focus, didn't we say earlier?

Where the young differ from their thoroughbred Hyderabadi parents is in their lack of 'take it easy attitude'. While the older lot was content with what they had, the new generation is hell-bent on taking it to another level. Most of them travel abroad for higher studies with their parents help, or the bank's, but study abroad is a definite must. The rest go to IITs, IIMs, and Hyderabad's very own ISB (Indian School of Business). Even if they're sure to inherit billions worth of family businesses. Contributing big time to this massive change are global exposure and external influences in the form of the IT revolution.

Hundreds of young professionals are pouring into the city thanks to the Microsofts, Googles and GEs setting up their Indian offices this side of the Vindhyas. Says Shankar Krishnamurthy, owner of Fusion 9, Grill Room and Deli 9, the city's fine dining restaurants: '22-25 year-olds spend much more than the older lot on dining. They want the best of wines and the best of food. They know all good things cost and they're willing to pay the price.' Plunging necklines and rising hemlines give way to business suits as young women occupy their hard earned positions in a boardroom. So, while you have a 25 something Srikala Reddy owning a nightclub and giving others in her business a run for their money, you also have the 25-year-old Teja Raju at the helm of Maytas, the real estate offshoot of Satyam, the IT bigwig and the Jethwani brothers in the jewellery and designer-wear business, Cherry Pestonji of Chermas, Upasna Kamineni of Apollo Hospitals – all in their 20s, running empires and having fun while at it.

Pockets are getting deeper; life is being lived like it is meant to be. 'Weddings are becoming bigger,' says Dinaz Noria, the city's celebrity designer wedding-planner. 'Today's girls and boys go to great lengths to make sure their once-in-a-lifetime (hopefully!) event is special in all aspects. They know their mind. They participate at every stage of the planning. Even if their parents are involved, major decisions are taken by the young bride and groom. The best part is they don't pinch pennies.'

So what happens when lavish weddings don't turn into happy ever after? Divorce, what else? No mud slinging, no character assassination, limited courtroom appearances. Sometimes people around don't even get to know of the divorce until one asks: 'So, how's your other half.' And the young girl/guy answers: 'We are not together any more.' And if you say 'what?' in shock, you'll get a self-assured, 'It wasn't working out. We're divorced now.' Sometimes in less than a year. Are patience levels getting lower and values going out of the window? 'Not really,' says Shravya, whose marriage lasted less than a year, 'you don't have to check the whole container to see if the rice is cooked. One grain should do.' So there. No more enduring till the wound gets chronic and the pain lasts a lifetime.

Another aspect that has undergone a tremendous change is the look of buildings. With so many offshore companies setting up shop in the city's Hitech City, the IT Mecca, anybody who drives through the area can't believe they are in erstwhile Hyderabad. You could be in Singapore, Malaysia or even the US. The city's architectural landscape has opened the eyes of many non-Hyderabadis. Even homes look different now. Till recently, Hyderabadis couldn't relate to apartment culture. After much resistance, they have succumbed to the housing demand and escalating land rates, and one finds high rises mushrooming in and around the city. Fortunately, some areas like Jubilee Hills are protected from the onslaught of modern-day wonders and still retain the charm of homes with gardens.

Hyderabadis are all over the place now. Everywhere in the world. Across continents, countries, prairies, deserts, great lakes, green forests, islands. Everywhere. The Hyderabadi diaspora continues to expand just as the city stretches from Shamshabad to Shamirpet today. From films to sports. A long way from where it started. But, as we never tire of reminding the rest of the world and ourselves – once a Hyderabadi, always a Hyderabadi. So, they keep coming back to find old haunts gone, buildings pulled down and turned into malls and multiplexes, homes razed and converted into three-hundred and fifty flats on five hundred yards and being sold at exorbitant rates.

Well, well, times they are changing. Luckily for us, our love for food remains untouched. In fact, nobody can escape the magic of Hyderabadi cuisine. Mouth-watering Shahi Cuisine of Hyderabad. Most slim Sultanas and beefcake Pashas believe in starving themselves and saving their appetites for biryani. Speaks volumes about how some things have remained untouched. Even today, Hyderabad's young believe in upholding traditions when it comes to eating. Several young people belonging to Muslim families irrespective of gender have learnt the Hyderabadi art of entertaining on Dastarkhan.

The 400 years of Hyderabadi culture that has its origin in art, music, dance, and poetry is most popular for its cuisine. Hyderabad is never complete without the mention of the *Shahi Dastarkhan*. The Dastarkhan is the dining place where the food is served and eaten. It is normally a low *chowki* for the dining table and cotton mattresses for squatting and bolsters for the backrest. The Dastarkhan holds a place of reverence in every household.

What makes the Hyderabadi cuisine special is the use of special ingredients, carefully chosen and cooked to the right degree. The addition of a certain herb, spice, condiment, or an amalgam of these adds a unique taste and texture. The herbs and spices used and the method of preparation gives the dish its name. *Murgh do pyaza* gets its name from the onions that are added twice to the dish in two variations. The *masalas* or the rich blend of herbs, spices and condiments give the dishes a base, or what is popularly known as 'gravy'. Some of these blends are well-kept secrets that only pass down the family line or from the *ustad* (teacher) to *shagird* (pupil). The head cooks or the *khansamas* were an asset to the household, and were treated with due respect.

The word *Nawabi* is as synonymous with the Hyderabadi cuisine as *Shahi* is with Lucknowi. These terms conjure delicacies that are rich in taste and texture with mouth-watering aromas. The *kebabs* in Hyderabad need a special mention; the *shammi kebab* is one such popular dish. The kebabs are originally from Greece! The Hyderabadi meal is never complete without the bread from the kilns of the local bakers. The breads from this cuisine are equally popular, be it rich *sheermal* or *lukmi* (bread stuffed with savory mince meat). Bread is not only an accompaniment to the meal but also forms a base for a popular sweet dish *Double ka Meetha*.

Hyderabad's strong Mughlai influence is perhaps one reason why the Hyderabadi biryani has become so popular all over India. This famous dish has been experimented with time and again to a perfection. In fact the biryani has influenced the Hyderabadi's tongue so strongly that other famous dishes of Hyderabad usually take a back seat. It takes an extraordinary taste for other dishes to beat the competition of biryani.

Thank the stars that the winds of change haven't altered the yearnings of the palate. If anything, they have been fanned.

So what else has remained unchanged? The warmth of the soul, the hospitality, the tendency to trust and good old Hyderabadi Urdu. *Kaiku* hasn't become *kyun* and *nakko* hasn't yet changed to *nahin*. Thankfully, not yet. Like they say, you can take a Hyderabadi out of Hyderabad but not Hyderabad out of a Hyderabadi. Says Imtiyaz, a businessman, 'Recently at an immigration queue in Heathrow I had these two suited, booted gentlemen with their short skirt, streaked hair women standing ahead of me. I passed them off as *angrez* from the way they looked. Their complexions, English accent and so on. Until one of them, impatient with the delay, burst out "Kithi der lagarein ji in logan. India say kharab hai bhosdikay. (How long are these guys taking? It's worse than India".' No English equivalent for the last word). Nothing like chaste Hyderabadi to de-stress. Only a Hyderabadi can relate to that.